Teaching Techniques for Communicative English

by Jane Revell

Essential Language Teaching Series

General Editor: Roger H. Flavell

MODERN ENGLISH
PUBLICATIONS

To my Mother and Father

First published 1979
Reprinted 1983, 1984 (twice), 1986, 1987, 1988, 1990 (twice), 1991

Published by *Macmillan Publishers Ltd*
London and Basingstoke

ISBN 0–333–27177–7

Illustrations Brian Roll

Printed in Hong Kong

Acknowledgements

I should like to acknowledge my special indebtedness to Hugh L'Estrange who read this book and made lots of useful suggestions (and who also helped out with the typing when one finger proved too slow!) .

I should also like to thank Frances Newman and John Johnson of Kingsway-Princeton College of Further Education, London for their excellent ideas (see particularly pages 76 and 69) and also Dr David Thomas of the University of Bristol, Department of Drama.

The Author and Publishers wish to acknowledge the following illustration sources. They have tried to contact the copyright holders but where they may have failed will be pleased to make the necessary arrangements at the first opportunity.

Jim Brownbill 32 and 89
Christiane Charillon 68 and 69
Crown Copyright C.O.L. 31
Ford of Gt. Britain 87
Fougasse/Hodder and Stoughton 67
Keystone Press Agency 31
London Transport 71
Metropolitan Police 32
National Westminster Bank Ltd. 79

Preface

I am a teacher of English as a foreign language and at the moment I am learning German as a foreign language in what I would say is a very 'non-communicative' way. For three whole hours every morning we listen to the teacher explain rule after rule before we move on to apply these rules in exercise after exercise in the book. In the street after the lesson, I need to know where the 53 bus stops. There is a lady coming. By the time I have managed to formulate my question in German, the lady has gone past. I ask the next passer-by, and expect short and easy-to-follow directions. Instead he says in German, 'Oh you've just missed one. Actually I'm going towards the Haus der Kunst, so I could give you a lift if you like. My car's right over there.' 'Wie bitte?!' (Pardon?). I am unable to communicate successfully in German, even on a very simple level. Why? For the reasons, let's go back to the classroom.

In my German class I normally get to say something about once every hour, when I read out a sentence from an exercise or text. I always talk to the teacher and never to any of the other students, and I never decide what to say, as it's written in the book for me. No wonder when I come out to face the real world I am thrown! It's true that this is a very extreme example, and luckily, because I am living in Germany and surrounded by German, my German lessons are unlikely to be a permanent obstacle to successful communication in the language. For foreign learners of English outside an English-speaking environment however, the problem could be a very serious one.

In coping with a foreign language, confidence plays a very large part. A student needs to feel that he will be able to apply what he has learnt in the classroom to real life, and be able to tackle many different situations in a foreign language in a foreign country. It is up to the teacher to give the students this confidence, by providing plenty of opportunities for them to practise what they have learnt in as realistic a way as possible inside the classroom.

Very often teachers are tied to a specific book and are aiming to get their students through an exam which tests specific items in that book. Even in this situation, which is far from ideal, there is room for 'communicative' activities, activities in which the students can transfer their learning to real situations. Suppose the teacher is working with Alexander's 'First Things First' at Lesson 77, for example. Rather than just practise everything in the way suggested in the Teacher's Book and move quickly on to the next lesson, the teacher might think about an activity where the students can practise the structures they have learnt (I want to . . . and, Can't you wait till . . . ?) in a similar situation, but in a way which allows them to think and to use language more creatively. They could work in pairs, for example, one as the receptionist, who has some pages from a diary in which certain days and times are booked up, and one as the person who wants to make the appointment. Between them they must work out a suitable time.

The activities described on the following pages are of this type. They can be used on their own or they can be used alongside any standard textbook and slotted in at appropriate moments to provide a 'transfer' stage in the lesson. They are activities, (particularly the later ones), designed to give learners a chance to experiment with their new linguistic skills, to be more creative. Activities, in short, to bridge the gap between 'skill-getting' in the classroom and 'skill-using' in real life.

Contents

1 Communication

1.1 Surprises

Communication is an exchange between people, of knowledge, of information, of ideas, of opinions, of feelings. It takes place in a multitude of ways, from the writings of the weightiest tome to the merest flicker of an eyelid. For genuine communication to take place, what is being communicated must be something new to the recipient: there is no sense in him being able to tell in advance what is going to happen. Communication is full of surprises. It is this element of unexpectedness and unpredictability which makes communication what it is, and for which it is so hard to prepare the student by conventional teaching methods.

It is true that there are a few fairly predictable responses: 'Hello' will produce one of a limited number of predictable replies, 'Hello', 'Hi', 'Good morning', etc. But these exchanges take place in a very small number of special situations – they are often social formulae, which serve to establish or maintain relations between the speakers rather than convey any earth-shattering information!

It is also true that we can often predict the semantic area of a response and even guess at key words which will come up. If, after a visit to the zoo, someone asks, 'Did you see the reptiles?', the response is likely to be in the general area of 'zoo-going' and animals, and words such as 'snake', 'lizard' and 'crocodile' might well occur.

In a lot of cases, however, responses are completely un-predictable. The question 'Did you see the reptiles?' could produce any of the following replies:

'You bet we did. At £1.60 to go in, we made sure we got our money's worth!'

'That reminds me, did you ring Aunt Nelly?'

'Oh, have you heard about John going to Kenya?' etc.

This sort of interaction is very often ignored in language teaching.

Until fairly recently the emphasis in TEFL was on the formation of language habits rather than on the development of communicative skills. Stimulus/response drills and the like encourage learners to think that any given utterance has a set reply. Although this type of classroom exercise is valuable practice in formulating communications and 'getting the tongue round' stretches of language, it is a means to an end rather than an end in itself, and the transfer to real life is not automatic: an intermediate stage is called for. The sort of activities described in subsequent chapters of the book, (see particularly Chapter 4), are designed to help bridge this gap.

1.2 Communication

We use language to communicate. We do not just communicate facts to each other, we always convey what we feel about those facts – finding a completely neutral statement is impossible. If I say 'It's raining', the listener will know whether I'm surprised (because the sun was shining only ten minutes ago), or whether I'm upset (because we were going to have a picnic), or whether I'm relieved (because the hockey match will be cancelled) and so on, and the clues he will use to deduce this will not necessarily be verbal ones. Words are used to communicate propositions. Words **can** also convey attitudes, but more often than not, attitudes are conveyed by intonation, gesture, facial expression and many other non-verbal means. To quote Abercrombie (1963:70), '. . . although our vocal organs are enough for the mere production of speech sounds, it is hardly an exaggeration to say that we need our entire bodies when we converse'. Meaning is conveyed not only through language, but also through bodily contact, physical proximity, orientation, bodily posture, gesture, head-nods, facial expression, eye movement and even appearance. Also important are the non-linguistic aspects of speech: the speed at which a person speaks, how loud or how softly he speaks, the pitch and the quality of his voice (whether husky, whispered, strident, etc), all these things contribute to the meaning of the actual words said. La Barre's work on gesture (1972) seems to prove that this is both specific to certain cultures and arbitrary (and therefore needs to be taught), rather than universal and instinctive. We may think that everybody uses a finger to point at something like we do, but the American Indians, for example, point with their lips. When a Masai spits, it is a sign of affection, not of contempt. The Basuto hiss to applaud, the Japanese to show respect to a social superior. While Westerners stand up to show their respect, Fijians and Tongans sit down. Even very widespread gestures like nodding the head to mean 'yes' and shaking it to mean 'no' are not totally universal: the Anin in Japan, the Semang in Malaya and the Ethiopians all use different gestures to indicate 'yes' and 'no'. There are also wide cultural differences when it comes to bodily contact and physical proximity. While Latin peoples tend to stand very close to the person they're talking to and often touch each other in the course of a conversation, Northern Europeans prefer to keep a greater distance between speakers and very rarely touch each other.

These things then need to be learnt, to prevent misunderstandings arising. Students need to be able to communicate not only propositions, but also the attitude that is appropriate to what they are saying. It is not being advocated that learners become proficient in non-verbal communication at the expense of their linguistic skills, even though it's quite possible to make yourself understood on certain matters simply by grunting and waving your arms about! Verbal and non-verbal aspects of communication should interrelate in a teaching programme, and some of the activities suggested later have been designed with this in mind.

1.3 Communicative competence

In 1965 the American linguist Noam Chomsky made a distinction very similar to the one that Ferdinand de Saussure had made between 'langue' and 'parole' in 1916. The distinction made by Chomsky was between 'competence' – a speaker's intuitive knowledge of the rules of his native language – and 'performance' – what he actually produces by applying these rules. Chomsky was talking about *grammatical* rules: a native speaker, he said, knows intuitively which sentences are grammatical, and which are not, and it is his linguistic competence which tells him this. So far so good, but many linguists (among them Hymes, Gumperz and Halliday) came to feel that Chomsky didn't go far enough: his 'ideal speaker-listener in a completely homogeneous speech community' (1965:3) took no account whatever of any socio-cultural features, of the fact that we talk to different people, in different situations, about different things.

In 1970, Campbell and Wales proposed that the Chomskyan notion of competence should be extended beyond purely grammatical competence to include a more general communicative ability. Language does not occur in isolation, as Chomsky seems to suggest; it occurs in a social context and reflects social rather than linguistic purposes. A child acquires a knowledge of sentences not only as grammatical, but also as appropriate to the context in which they are made. 'He knows when and when not to speak, what to talk about with whom, when, where, and in what manner'. (Hymes 1972:277) He has *communicative* competence as well as linguistic competence. There are many different ways of saying the same thing – of asking someone to be quiet, for example, (see page 29) – and we choose one rather than another according to the criterion of 'appropriateness' to the situation.

Theories of communicative competence imply that teachers must do more than just supply learners with a number of language structures to manipulate. There are cases of people being unable to use a language after years of formal teaching: 'Foreign language cripples with all the necessary muscles and sinews, but unable to walk alone'. (Rivers 1972:72) Teachers must demonstrate how language items are used, and in what situations they are appropriate. They must show learners that a *choice* of words is possible, indeed necessary, and will colour the propositional content of what they say. They must teach them, in short, the 'use' of language as well as its 'usage'. (Widdowson 1978:3)

1.4 Teaching communicative competence

The crucial question is how to bridge the gap between linguistic competence and communicative competence, how to develop a smooth transition between 'skill-getting' and 'skill-using'. (Rivers 1973:25) Rivers warns that a schizophrenic situation can develop between these two types of activity: in 'skill-getting' the emphasis is on the going, not on the destination, whereas in 'skill-using' students are aiming at the goal of communicative competence. The gap is so difficult to bridge because the classroom environment by its very nature makes genuine communication extremely elusive: as we have already said, communication stems from necessity, and this element is usually absent in a classroom situation. A student often knows in advance what he will say and what everybody else will say too. He and everybody else (including the teacher) asks questions to which they already know the answer:

T (Referring to a picture or a text) Ask what Johnny was doing at 3 o'clock yesterday.

S1 What was Johnny doing at 3 o'clock yesterday?

S2 He was sitting under a banana tree.

Nobody is exchanging any information, and consequently nobody really needs to listen to what is being said. The element of choice talked about in the last section is missing – there is too much control, there are no surprises. Necessity, in the form of doubt, of unpredictability, of an 'information gap', can however be created in the classroom by the use of activities where the participants are only in possession of *part* of the total information. Students then have a certain amount of choice in what to say, they ask questions because they don't know the answer, and they have a reason for listening to one another.

'Jigsaw' listening or reading is one way of providing an information gap: each student, or group of students, has one section of the whole tape or text, or certain bits of information that the others don't have, and they must swap ideas and information in order to discover the whole.* Activities where one person, or half the class, has all the information, and the rest none, also make for 'authentic' communication: those 'in the know' must give instructions to those 'in the dark'. Someone, for example, might have a geometric design and must give the others precise instructions for drawing exactly the same thing.

---

* The book by Geddes and Sturtridge in the Practical Material section (page 94) is based on this idea.

Or, using Lego, one group of students could give another instructions to make a specific model.

'Language in action' is advocated by Ure (1969) to bridge the gap: scientific experiments, making things, assembling component parts of a puzzle, and exercises such as describing the differences between a corkscrew and a bottle-opener. All these activities are recorded and compared with a native speaker's performance, so that learners can gradually build up a 'native speaker-type intuition'. (Broughton 1978:253) Sandra Savignon (1972) takes a slightly more radical view. She feels that experience in 'authentic' communication should not be delayed until the learner has a basic set of grammatically correct sentences. Trial and error learning should be used straight away: skill-getting is achieved *through* skill-using. Her students (English speakers learning French) are introduced to simple kinds of role-play activity very early on. They might enact a situation in English on greetings, for example, watch the same situation enacted in French by native speakers, and then discuss the differences. They then re-enact the situation in English using French gesture before moving on to try it entirely in French (verbally *and* non-verbally). Needless to say they have to learn a lot of useful expressions – 'Je ne comprends pas', 'Comment dit-on?', 'Eh bien', 'truc', 'machin', etc – right from the start.

What I would suggest for bridging the skill-getting and skill-using gap are activities where learners are 'playing a part' in situations which are not predictable – e g role-play (see page 60).

1.5 Accuracy versus fluency

Teaching communicative competence means a reassessment of our attitude towards error. Having decided that perfection at the pattern drill level is not enough, and that communicative competence is our goal, are we going to allow our learners to make mistakes? And if so, to what extent and of what kind?

In recent years there has been a swing away from the idea that every mistake should be stamped out immediately or else the student will develop bad habits which are then impossible to get rid of. Making mistakes is now considered to be a necessary part of a foreign learner's progress towards mastery of the language, or his . . . 'interlanguage' (Selinker 1972), the sum total of his knowledge of the language at any given moment, which is constantly changing. It is thought that these mistakes will right themselves in the normal process of things as the learner receives more information. They will not right themselves however unless the learner is encouraged to test out the hypotheses he is continually making about the new language, that is, unless he is given the opportunity to make mistakes. When a learner acquires a new word or structure or function, he can only find out what the boundaries of its use are by trying it out in different contexts. If he is always terrified of making a mistake, he will never really come to master that piece of language but only have a partial understanding of it. Students then should be encouraged to try out language without the fear of being shouted at if they happen to be wrong. This type of 'hypothesis-testing' mistake must of course be corrected so that the learner can widen or narrow boundaries, but this needn't be done on the spot (see page 13). Emphasis on correct production at all times can lead to serious inhibitions in the learner.

While I do not agree that learners should be actively encouraged to make mistakes in the way that Savignon suggests (see page 7), I feel that once students have had an opportunity to practise a new bit of language in a fairly controlled way, they should be able to try it out on their own without too much interference from the teacher. This calls for a good deal of sensitivity on the part of the teacher as to when and how to correct (see page 13).

Not only did the audio-lingual approach to English teaching lay emphasis on eliminating rank error, but it was also guilty of a failure to make clear that a grammatically correct sentence is not necessarily 'good' in a particular context (see page 5). It may be that this type of error of appropriateness is also a natural development in the learner's interlanguage. It is less likely to occur however if the teacher makes it clear when presenting new material in what situation the particular language item is appropriate.*

(NB The terms 'error' and 'mistake' are used here in their widest sense, as synonyms, and not in the way that P Corder uses them. (1973:259))

---

* Another book in this series, by John Norrish, is devoted to the subject of errors and what to do about them. In it there is a detailed discussion of the issues raised here.

2 Limbering up

2.1 Getting in the mood

In this chapter we shall be looking at activities for the classroom which encourage students to communicate with one another in the way that I have suggested is desirable. All of these
ideas have actually been used with foreign learners – most of
them with adults, and one or two of them with children – and
they have worked successfully.

Activities involving simulation and role-play (see Chapter 4)
require a certain amount of psychological preparation: there is a
need to break the students in gently, and gradually overcome
any inhibitions that they may quite naturally feel.

Although most *young* children seem to take to role-play
activities like ducks to water, some adult students who have
never done anything quite like it, and many adolescent students,
are less enthusiastic. They are afraid of being made to look silly
in front of their fellow-students, and exposed to their criticism.
A teacher who rushes into this type of activity without adequate
preparation exercises runs the risk of scaring his students off for
good. Building up the students' confidence, creating an atmosphere of trust (see page 16), teaching the students to relax – all
these things take time, and demand exercises where the indi-
viduals in a class are working together, getting to know each
other well. The activities in this chapter are designed to have this
effect, and include games, group and pair exercises intended to
'loosen up' the class, and create a relaxed and harmonious

atmosphere conducive to role-play activities. Even physical exercises are mentioned: they relax a person physically and so make him less inhibited generally. The exercises described in this chapter should be used over a period of time – one or two of them could be brought into every lesson.

2.2 Problems

Before describing the activities, I should like to mention two difficulties that can arise.

The first problem is a physical one: in classrooms with fixed desks all facing forwards in rows, group-work is difficult, and having people move around is even more difficult. If teaching is to be truly communicative then it almost goes without saying that the teacher should not be the focus of attention all the time, (as in Figure 1) but that the interaction should be general. Seating the students in a large circle (as in Figure 2) facilitates things: every student is in contact with both the teacher and every other student, and a large space is left in the middle for activities that require a lot of room.

Not:

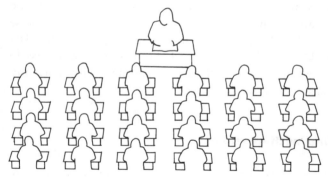

Figure 1

but:

Figure 2

The second problem is one of discipline, if the learners are not adults. This can be a very serious problem and often deters teachers from embarking on a noisy and potentially riotous activity! Three points could be mentioned here. Firstly, the physical grouping of the class is an important factor, and the circular arrangement suggested above does seem to give the teacher more control than other groupings – there is no-one he can't see easily! Also of prime importance is motivation: students who are interested in what is going on in the classroom and who find it relevant, realistic and fun will be less likely to cause trouble. Thirdly, the gradual build-up advocated in the last section should make it easier for all the members of a class to participate and to relate well to one another. This harmony tends to work against trouble-makers.

2.3 Dealing with mistakes

We have already talked about the treatment of error (see page 9) and have decided to go for fluency rather than accuracy in communicative language practice. The students will probably make quite a few mistakes, so what should a teacher do when, having vowed not to interfere, he hears a mistake that makes his hair stand on end?

There are ways of dealing with these 'bad' mistakes without disrupting the activity and alarming the student concerned.

Mario Rinvolucri advocates 'hot correction' in group work: he slips a piece of paper to the student with the correction written on it – he feels that if he leaves it until later the student will have forgotten what it was all about. Even this tends to be a little disruptive at first, although it is much less so with a group of students who are really used to the technique.

The teacher can also keep a note of any mistakes he hears, and go through them with individual students when the activity has finished. If several students are making the same mistake, it is worth planning a follow-up lesson to deal with the point.

Possibly the best method though, is to record the activity, using video or sound tape, and play it back to the students. The playback is both enjoyable and profitable as it normally provokes a good deal of discussion. Students can make suggestions themselves as to what they should or might have said in those circumstances. It is worthwhile teaching the students to use the equipment so that they are able to record themselves. With only one tape-recorder in the class, the groups will have to take it in turns to make recordings. Clearly in these circumstances the more tape-recorders the teacher can get hold of, the better.

2.4 'Getting to know you' games

1   One way of learning names is for the students to sit in a large circle or semi-circle. One person introduces himself. The person next to him must repeat the name and then introduce himself.

His neighbour must in turn repeat the names that have gone before, and then say his own name. And so on round the group.

A I'm Paul.

B Paul, I'm Sheila.

C Paul, Sheila, my name's Fred.

D Paul, Sheila, Fred, I'm Ethel.

2 Once they have introduced themselves to one another, the students stand in a circle. One person has a large ball. He throws this to someone in the circle, saying that person's name as he does so. If he gets the name right, the game continues in this way. If not, he must take the ball back and throw it again (not necessarily to the same person).

3 Students walk around the room looking at each other, trying to remember as much as possible about the other students' appearance. After two or three minutes they are asked to stand back to back with the nearest person, and to describe what he or she is wearing and what they look like (possibly aided by questions from that person). (Maley & Duff 1977: 23)

4 Students work in pairs, asking each other questions about their general background (interests, job, etc). The aim is to find out as much as possible about the other person in a given time, say 5 minutes, and then report back to the class (or group, if the class is a very large one) on their findings. This activity can be done with the aid of a questionnaire (see page 42). The teacher could also write cues up on the blackboard to guide students into asking the right sort of questions. For example: Home Family Job Hobbies Ambition etc.

5 Each student has half of a sentence. He must find the other half, and together with the person who has it, build up a short dialogue which incorporates the whole sentence:

Could you tell me	the way to the station?
My cat has just	eaten Mrs Denner's parrot.
I wonder if you	could give me a hand?
If I were you	I'd have it out!

With more advanced students, proverbs or idioms could be used for a change:

I was only pulling	your leg.
Get it off	your chest.
Let me twist	your arm.
Don't turn up	your nose.

6 Students are given a card on which there is a description along the following lines:

Your name is Pat.

You are a teacher.

You drive a Mini.

You belong to the ski club.

You like eating out, dancing, skiing.

You read a lot of science-fiction.

Most of the cards differ from each other by *one* item, but some-one somewhere has an *identical* card. In a class of 16, for example, there will be eight pairs of playing cards. Students must find their identical 'twin' by going around asking everybody questions beginning with 'What . . .?' The students may have to go through several questions before they discover that that person is not their 'twin'.

7 Each student is given a card with an utterance which would typically be said by a person in a specific profession:

Just a couple of fillings. (Dentist)

Your plugs need cleaning. (Garage mechanic)

There's a fault in the earth. (Electrician)

He must go round and find others who have things that would also be said by the same person in the course of his work. (The profession is not, of course, marked on the card.) 'Just a couple of fillings' might, for example, team up with 'Open wide, please' and 'Do you clean them last thing at night?' but not with 'Fried or grilled?' (At least we hope not!) This is a good technique for getting students to form new groups, especially if they have a tendency to mix only with people that they know, and it can be used over and over again.

Actual physical contact with others in a group can sometimes help in building up the atmosphere of trust and confidence that we have already emphasised (see page 10). The next three ideas involve touch, and can be used initially to try and overcome students' inhibitions and get them to feel more 'at home' with their fellow-students.

8 Groups of students hold hands in a circle. By going over, under and round their neighbours, without letting go of anyone, they gradually tie themselves in one big knot. The one student in each group who has not been participating must then unravel them. This he does by giving them instructions. They should also make suggestions which will help him.

9 One person stands with his eyes closed, in the middle of a group of three or four people who are quite close to him. He must let himself fall gently in any direction. The person on that side of him is to push him gently back and over to someone else, who in turn pushes him in another direction. This continues for about thirty seconds to one minute. The idea is to build up the middle person's trust in his fellow students.

10 Working in groups of three, the students must form themselves to look like various objects such as a tree or a telephone. It's important that the three should work as a group to form one telephone, rather than three individual telephones. The class then judges which is the most realistic or most imaginative object. Other objects which lend themselves well to this activity include: a bicycle, a teapot, a tap, a ladder and a clock. The students could also be left to decide on their own objects, and have the rest of the class guess what it is.

2.5 Activities 1: Gesture and mime

We have already said that when we communicate we use both verbal and non-verbal means (see pages 2 and 3), but teachers and textbooks of English have tended to concentrate exclusively on the former. The activities described below are intended to incorporate the non-verbal aspects of communication into the teaching programme by giving students an opportunity to learn and practise gestures, facial expressions and other 'para-linguistic' ways of communicating.

1 Students interpret various gestures or facial expressions that the teacher makes, for example, beckoning, nodding, winking, and so on. Where they would convey the same meaning with a different gesture, the students can demonstrate this. Apart from those already mentioned, the following gestures are interesting ones to try out:
Shaking your head
Pointing at something
Shrugging your shoulders
Waving goodbye
Giving a thumbs up (or down) sign
Putting your finger to your lips – Sh!
Hissing
Catching the attention of the waiter
Making a V-sign

Needless to say, this can be a really fascinating activity, especially with a multilingual class.

2   Students must get a message across to a person on the other side of the room, without using any words, as if they were at a crowded and noisy party. The teacher gives a card with a message on it to a student, who must then use nothing but gesture and mime to make himself understood. The other student(s) must interpret the message, which could be something like:
It's time to go.
There's a phone call for you.
Your slip's showing.
I'm having a terrible time.
I need something to eat.

3   What's my line? One student mimes an action that is typical of the job he does. The other students must then find out exactly what his job is by asking him questions to which he can only answer 'yes' or 'no'. They are allowed only ten questions. Cues can be put on the blackboard to help the students:
Uniform?
Regular hours?
Outside?
Common job?
Normally done by men?
Well-paid? etc
'This is the job he had last year' will elicit questions in the past tense, just as 'This is the job he's just been offered' will elicit questions in the future tense, should the teacher want to focus on a particular tense. 'Have (got) to' is another structure which can easily be practised in playing this game.

4   Pass the parcel. The students sit in a circle. The teacher gives every *other* student a card with the name of an object (always the

same object). This imaginary object is then passed around the circle. The half of the class who know what the object is must give the other half of the class visual and verbal clues (without actually naming the object) so that they can guess what it is. They must, for example, hold it in a certain way, and say things like: 'Careful! Don't squeeze it!' or 'It's still a bit hot' or 'If you hold her like that, she'll scratch you!'

5 Students are divided into groups of four or five. One, a guest staying at a hotel, is given a card on which is written something he wants or needs. He has a very bad cold and has lost his voice, so he must make himself understood to the others in the group – the collective hotel receptionist – entirely by the use of mime.

For elementary students it is enough that they grasp the general idea of what the hotel guest is trying to get across. More advanced students should be asked to produce the *exact* words written on the card. The reason for this is that it forces them to find synonyms for words and to search for different ways of saying the same thing. In trying to guess 'Could you tell me how to get to the cathedral?' for example, the students might well come up with any of the following things:

'Where's the cathedral, please?'

'Which way is the cathedral?'

'What's the best way to get to the cathedral?'

'Could you tell me the way to the cathedral?'

'I'm looking for the cathedral. Can you help me?'

'Do you know the way to the cathedral?'

'I wonder if you could tell me where the cathedral is?' etc

Some suggestions are given below for the sorts of things that might be written on cards:

Where is the nearest underground station?

Could you call me at 7.15 tomorrow, please?

Is there a cheap Indian restaurant near here?

I was very cold last night. Could I possibly have an extra
blanket tonight?
My room is too noisy.
Do you sell postcards?
Is it possible to make a phone call to Ireland from here?
The hot tap in my room isn't working.
Is there a doctor in the hotel?
Could you tell me how to get to the cathedral?
(Maley & Duff 1977:26)

6   The teacher mimes a short story:

He is woken up in the middle of the night by a noise downstairs. He is terrified – thinks it must be a burglar. Finally he
plucks up courage – gets out of bed puts on his dressing-gown
and slippers – takes a torch – creeps downstairs. He flings open
the door, and discovers . . . the cat.

When the teacher has finished the mime, the students must
recount the story. He can re-mime those parts that led to a variety
of interpretations or that the students didn't understand. Students should also be given the opportunity to mime their own
stories, possibly miming something that has actually happened
to them. Children in particular seem to love doing this, but
contrary to popular belief, adult groups will also enter happily
into the spirit of the thing given the right sort of classroom
atmosphere that we have talked about before. Students can work
individually, or in pairs or groups to act out a story on a certain
theme such as 'A Terrible Day' or 'A Strange Encounter', which
the other students then interpret.

7   With fairly advanced students, a form of 'Charades' using
proverbs or expressions can be played. The class is divided into
two teams. The teacher gives a card with an expression on it to
one member of a team, having first shown the other team what is
written on the card. The person with the card must use mime

and gesture to convey to his team-mates exactly what is written on the card. He can do this by miming the general meaning of the expression, or by miming the literal meaning of the individual words. Once his team have got the expression or proverb, they must explain what it means. Points are scored both for guessing what is written on the card within a certain time (say two minutes), and for correct explanations. Because expressions are so numerous, it is a good idea to use a definite theme for each game. Colours, for example, or animals:

Tell a white lie	Take the bull by the horns
Paint the town red	Flog a dead horse
Scream blue murder	Have a bee in one's bonnet
Catch someone red-handed	Go to the dogs
Be in someone's black books	Smell a rat
Be in the pink	Keep the wolf from the door

8 Auditions. Students are told that the director of a play is looking for a cast. He needs, for example, a grumpy old man, an elegant lady, a shy parish priest, a neurotic chain-smoking poet, etc. Students have to audition for the different parts using both speech and mime, and the class decides who should be given each one.

9 In order to help students build up characters as a preliminary to role-play proper, the teacher asks them to imagine they are a certain type of person and uses questions to enable them to think themselves into the part. A beggar, for example:
Are you male or female? Disabled or well? How long have you been a beggar? Where do you live? What do you eat? Have you got any friends? Any relations? Have you got a job? What are you wearing? How do you beg? What are the passers-by like? How do they treat you? etc
Groups of students could then mime short street scenes with the

beggar as the central figure, perhaps leading up to a dialogue between the beggar and a social worker, or a newspaper reporter asking passers-by their views on the problem and what they think should be done. (Adapted from Bruford 1958:83–84)

10 As the teacher reads a story, the students act it out. This is an activity more suitable for children, particularly those in the 8–12 age group, and a book that I have found very useful here is Leila Berg's 'Folk Tales, For Reading and Telling', (1976). The stories that work especially well are those with a lot of repetition such as, 'The Soup Stone' and 'Jack and his Friends'. After a while the children are able to join in the dialogue as well as just acting out the story. For certain stories the teacher may want to bring in props: 'The Soup Stone' requires a large pan, a spoon, a stone, a carrot, an onion, salt and pepper, and something that will stand in for a chicken if the teacher doesn't have one to hand! The text of certain stories may need to be edited or changed slightly, depending on the age and level of English of the class, as these stories were intended for native-speakers. If a teacher feels his class would find it too difficult to listen and act at the same time, the class could of course 'play' the story after he has finished reading, or during a second reading.

Adults *can* also do this type of activity, though suitable texts are not too easy to find. A running commentary on the arrival of a V I P at an airport, with students taking the parts of hosts, guests, airport officials, and even showing the reactions of the crowd, is a good exercise. (Dickinson et al 1976:183)

Perhaps a more suitable activity for adults is to have them finish a story, in words or mime, although the big advantage of the simultaneous 'listen and mime' is that the teacher can see immediately whether his students have understood or not. He can also see at a glance exactly *which* students have not quite got it.

2.6 Activities 2: intonation and expression

1 Students react to various items of news. They can react either vocally by making some sort of exclamation: Oo! Mm! Wow! etc, or verbally by using words: No! Really? My God! etc

Prince Philip has run off with Mrs Thatcher.

Tube fares are going up tomorrow.

The pubs are giving away free beer next Sunday.

There's been a mid-air collision in the States.

The bakers are out on strike.

Potatoes are down to 5p a pound.

Snow is on the way.

England are out of the World Cup.

Richard Burton and Liz Taylor are getting married again.

Chinese has been made the number 1 international language. Everyone should learn it.

An earthquake kills 1000 people in Turkey.

2 Students react vocally or verbally, and with gestures, to the following situations, so as to express:

Exasperation

   You've just got into the bath. The phone rings.

   After running up that hill . . . there goes the last bus!

   Having queued for two hours, you finally get to the box office. The last tickets have just been sold.

Pain

   You're chopping onions and you cut yourself.

   A wasp stings you on the neck.

   Making the tea, you pour boiling water all over your foot.

Delight

   You're given a tiny kitten to hold.

   You see Mount Everest for the first time.

   You've won the pools – half a million pounds.

Shock

Someone bursts a balloon right by your ear.

You come out of the sauna and take an icy cold shower.

You get to the cash desk in the supermarket. Your wallet's gone!

Disgust

You find a big black hairy spider in your bed.

As you dig into your salad you suddenly find a lot of maggots waving their heads about.

Walking barefoot, you step on a cockroach.

3 Students can be trained to distinguish polite from disinterested and rude intonation patterns by the use of mood cards as suggested by Brita Haycraft (1971:16). Students are asked (by the teacher or by another student) 'Would you like a chocolate?' (The teacher should actually have a bag of chocolates or sweets to offer the students.) If, when they say, 'Thank you', they sound rather off-hand because the first syllable is not pitched high enough, the teacher points to the grumpy mood card and says, '*This* is what you sound like'. Next he points to the smiling face and says, 'Try it *this* way'. Then he demonstrates the high fall for the students.

4 Three or four line dialogues which express feelings as well as facts provide excellent intonation practice. They are fun to do and are short enough to be easily remembered. The dialogue can be played first of all on a tape-recorder or, even simpler, the teacher can read it himself, taking both parts. The teacher can indicate when a different person is speaking by changing his voice slightly, by stepping to the left or right, by pointing to two pictures of people up on the blackboard, by using two different hats which he switches round very quickly, or by using puppets. When the students have heard the dialogue once or twice, they might be asked to repeat one of the parts after the teacher, in chorus and individually, while the teacher listens carefully to their intonation patterns. The teacher can then take one part of the dialogue, and the students the other. Next they copy the second part and at this stage the class can be divided – one half taking A's part, the other B's. Finally they split into pairs to practise the dialogue, by this time incorporating substitution words or phrases that they or the teacher have suggested and which have been written on the board, while the teacher goes round and listens in. Needless to say, this is by no means the only way of handling a short dialogue. It is hoped that the teacher will experiment and try out the many other possibilities that exist, and so give his class the variety of approach that a class needs. It is suggested, however, that this type of dialogue be used for no longer than ten minutes with a class. They are designed to provide short intensive practice of certain structures and intonation patterns, and can easily become boring if left to run on too long. Here are some examples:

a   A   Have you heard?

     B   No, what?

     A   *The Pope's dead!**

     B   Really? *How incredible!*†

     *Substitute:

     I passed my driving test.   Kevin got the job.

Betty's broken her leg.   Pamela's pregnant.
Manchester United won.   Jack got the sack, etc
†Substitute an appropriate exclamation:
How fantastic!   How awful!
How terrible!   How wonderful!
How amazing!   How surprising! etc

b   A   Have you *bought the batteries** yet?
      B   The batteries! I've been meaning to buy them, but I keep
             forgetting.
      A   Oh for Heaven's sake!
      *Substitute:
      Fed the cat   Told your mother
      Done the ironing   Written that letter
      Talked to Fred   Watered the plants etc

c   A   (*looks at his watch*) Oh! I've got to go.
      B   Have you? Can't you stay a bit longer?
      A   No, I've got to *meet Janet**.
      *Substitute:
      Go to the chemist's   Get some fish
      Finish an essay   Ring Robert
      Post a letter   Catch a bus

d   A   Is there any *coffee** left?
      B   Yes, there's lots. Would you like some more?
      A   Mmm. Yes please.
      *Substitute:
      Cake/Strawberries/Cream/Jelly/Peanuts/Chocolate, etc
      NB In this dialogue students must take care to use is/are
      in the appropriate places.

Where names of people are used in the dialogues above, it is
suggested that teachers use names of people who are actually
in the class or else of people who are known to the whole class
(other teachers, perhaps), and that they encourage the students

to do this too. It is far more relevant and interesting to talk about the real Betty who has really broken her leg than all the hypothetical Johns and Marys who are forever doing very boring things!

Short dialogues of this kind are very easy to write, but should the teacher want ready-made ones, Jerrom and Szkutnik 1965 and Ockenden 1972, (see Practical Material, page 94) are useful sources.

2.7 What would you say?

Reacting in an appropriate way to a situation can be quite a problem in a foreign language and students should be given plenty of opportunity to practise this skill, which is clearly very important in any social situation with English speakers. Furthermore, it is tested in the oral tests of several well-known examinations (Cambridge First Certificate and Proficiency, for example); for this reason alone many learners are keen to acquire it.

Appropriate responses can be taught by means of *verbal* or *visual* stimuli. This should be done gradually, starting with one or two words, then whole sentences, until students can maintain a complete dialogue.

USING A VERBAL STIMULUS

For teaching purposes one could divide the situations described into three categories. First, those situations that require a formulaic response, ie where the response is fairly standard and predictable. Second, situations that can be used to stimulate the use of a particular structure or function. And third, situations that concentrate on the choice of an appropriate response according to who is being addressed. A more detailed description of the situations, together with a number of examples of each, is set out on the following pages.

1 Situations requiring a set response.

What would you say when . . .

a Someone sneezes.

b You want to sit down at a table in a cafe, but are not sure whether the seat is free or not.

c You don't understand the word 'grotty'.

d You don't quite catch what someone says.

e You see that a woman is about to step off the pavement right in front of a bus.

f You accidentally bump into someone in the street.

g A friend says 'Thank you very much for your help'.

h A friend asks if he can use your phone.

i You are in a colleague's house and want to make a phone call.

j A friend tells you he's just passed his driving-test.

How and exactly when these formulae are taught must be left to the individual teacher. I mention them here to draw attention to their importance, and to the fact that they are very often overlooked. Some of them occur very frequently, in fact a student is almost certainly going to need examples c and d during his very first week of learning English. Having these formulae 'up his sleeve' will encourage the student to embark on longer stretches of dialogue, and will help in later role-play activities.

2 Situations to practise a specific structure, A or function, B.

A What would you say in the following situations, using either: I wonder if I could . . . ?

or: I wonder if you could . . . ?

a You bought a pair of shorts in Marks and Spencers and found they were too small. Take them back.

I wonder if I could . . . ?

b You're staying in a hotel and want breakfast in bed to-morrow.

I wonder if you could . . . ?

Once they have practised the structure once or twice, the students should be able to make an appropriate response to the situation without any cues from the teacher:

c Ring up your hairdresser for an appointment.

d You're in a restaurant. There's no menu on your table. The people at the next table have finished with theirs.

e You've got flu. A friend is going out shopping. You need some milk.

B Disagree mildly, eg 'Well I wouldn't go quite that far' or strongly, eg 'Rubbish! That's totally unfounded!' with the following statements . . .

a I think women are irrational.

b They're unable to think logically and objectively.

c They let their emotions rule their lives.

d They go on and on about something.

e And they all end up just like their mothers!

This type of contextualised drill gives the student a chance to concentrate on the function in question and learn to 'get his tongue round it' quickly. Once he can do this with ease, he is ready to incorporate it into a more extended dialogue, possibly using cue-cards or role-cards. The teacher should find it relatively easy to draw up groups of situations like these for himself, but if he is short of ideas there is no shortage of helpful textbooks which contain this type of exercise (see Practical Material, pages 93–95).

3 Situations which concentrate on the question of appropriateness.

A What would you say when . . .

a Two small children are making so much noise, that you can't hear the radio news?

b You're trying to study but your flat-mate is singing loudly in his bath?

c You're phoning someone in Canada and the secretaries in the office are talking and laughing?

d The neighbours' party is still in full swing. It's 4 o'clock in the morning?

e Your boss and his wife have arrived for dinner. They're in the hall. The baby's just fallen asleep?

B

Invite your	boss and his wife boyfriend old English teacher closest friend neighbours	for Sunday lunch.

In a similar situation – getting someone to make less noise or inviting people for lunch – the language used might be very dissimilar depending on who one is talking to, and exercises like these are designed to pinpoint these differences of register. In A, for example, the responses could range from 'For God's sake shut up!' to 'Could I ask you to be very quiet for a moment?' In B 'How about lunch on Sunday?' would be fine where friends are concerned, whereas a more appropriate way of inviting the old English teacher would be to say something like: 'I was wondering, if you weren't doing anything on Sunday, whether you'd like to come for lunch?' The teacher needs to make explicit these register differences and then give his class plenty of opportunities to practise them. They should be able to make a conscious choice about using one form rather than another because it is 'appropriate' in that situation. They should also learn that it is not enough to produce a form which is grammatically correct: if it is inappropriate, it is unacceptable.

USING A VISUAL STIMULUS

The pictures which follow are taken from magazines and are examples of the way in which magazine pictures can be used to stimulate and practise appropriate responses. In some of the pictures I have put a 'bubble' coming from one of the people to indicate that the student should practise an appropriate remark for that person. The teacher may choose to present the pictures like this or to encourage the students to become different characters in the scene.

3 From script to spontaneity

Many adult learners have already been taught English in a fairly formal way at school. They may have been given few opportunities in the classroom to actually get up and do things, and to express themselves freely in a foreign language. In fact they may have been actively discouraged from being imaginative and inventive, from having a go at saying something they want to say, and never mind the mistakes. They may be rather 'book dependent'. These students may understandably feel a little anxious about attempting less structured activities in English: they may not take kindly to having a role-card thrust into their hand the moment they set foot in the classroom and to being told to get on with it! What I would suggest is breaking them in gently by giving them fully scripted parts at first, to make them feel more secure. As the students progress they are required to supply more and more of the dialogue themselves, until finally they are interacting with each other with nothing but a photograph or a role-card to guide them.

3.1 Scripted and partially scripted dialogues

1   Sketches which are not too long and which involve plenty of repetition so as to make them easier to remember make good script material. All the better if they are funny and if strong feelings are expressed in them: students are often more prepared to let themselves go if they can hide behind an easily identifiable

caricature. Sketches can be used in class in much the same way as any other dialogue, together with a tape, but they also lend themselves very well to a team-teaching technique with two or three teachers acting out the sketch and basing further practice on it. The aim is to get the students to act out the sketches themselves, and they really seem to enjoy doing this once they are sufficiently familiar with the new material. A successful technique involves *not* allowing the students just to read out their lines. The students work in pairs or threes, depending on the number of parts. Whoever is going to speak must look down at his script and take in as much of his line as he can. He must then look up and, making eye contact with the person he is addressing (who should *not* have his head buried in his script, preparing *his* next line), he should deliver the line, or as much of it as he can remember. It certainly doesn't matter if students fail to produce the exact words in the script – indeed we hope that they will improvise as much as possible. This is in fact what tends to happen automatically with a class, but it should perhaps be made clear to them at the start. When they have practised a couple of times in pairs or threes, some students should be invited to act out the sketch for the rest of the class, and for this the teacher should have some props handy. For 'Anything to Declare?' (see page 35) a suitcase is basically all that's needed, together with one or two bottles (even milk bottles will do!) Students are usually very willing to donate a watch, and a necklace or bracelet or any other item of jewellery that they have.

The sketch which follows, 'Anything to Declare?' was written to reinforce a particular teaching point. It focuses on 'something/ nothing/anything' with some finer distinctions that can be made between them, and also touches on polite requests. This sketch has been used successfully with adult *and* adolescent learners (age 13/17) at intermediate level, ie learners who already have a basic knowledge of English.
Suggested procedure:

The teacher introduces the topic of the sketch: 'Have you ever had any problems going through Customs?'

Students see sketch 'live' or on video, or hear it on sound tape. Failing all those, they can be given the sketch to read.

The teacher checks understanding of the sketch by asking a few questions. The students might also have been asked to listen out for certain things *before* the first viewing/hearing: 'Notice how the Customs officer asks if the traveller has cigarettes, wine etc to declare. Why do you think he says it that way?' and the teacher should now go through these questions.

The sketch is played again, followed perhaps by a little practice on the key teaching points.

Scripts are given out, and the students practise in twos or threes in the way that has already been described. Before doing this they may like to 'shadow-read' their particular parts: the tape is played again and students read along with it, attempting to imitate the pace and the intonation of the speaker. (This exercise is not really feasible unless the sketch *is* on video or sound tape).

Students come out and act through the sketch, trying not to depend too much on the script.

Sketch 1   Anything to declare?
The customs hall at Gitwack airport. The passengers on the flight from Rome are going through customs.

C.O.*	Good evening, Madam. Have you got anything to declare?
Woman	No, nothing at all! Nothing at all!
C.O.	Come on now, Madam. Everybody's got something to declare.
Woman	Well *I* haven't got *anything* to declare.
C.O.	Have you read this notice?
Woman	Which notice? Oh that notice over there? Oh yes . . . hundreds of times.
C.O.	And you still say you've got nothing to declare?
Woman	Nothing.
C.O.	No cigarettes?
Woman	No. None at all. I don't smoke. Such a filthy habit.
C.O.	No wines? No spirits?
Woman	No. None at all. I don't drink. Not a drop.
C.O.	No fur coats?
Woman	No. None at all. I would never wear one. I *love* animals.
C.O.	No perfume?
Woman	(*with a large sigh*) Listen to me, young man. I get up at *five* every morning, I jog *five* times round the park before breakfast, I eat a banana for lunch, *and* I go to church on Sunday. I neither smoke, drink, wear fur coats nor use perfume. Do you understand?
C.O.	Well Madam, I'm afraid I must ask you to open your case anyway. Open your case.
	(*nothing happens*)
	Open your case please, Madam.
	(*still nothing happens*)
	Would you mind opening your case please, Madam?
Woman	Well . . . since you ask so nicely . . .
	(*sound of case being opened*)

* *Customs Officer*

	(sound of case being searched)
C.O.	Hello, hello, hello! What's this then? A gold watch, eh?
Woman	Oh that! That's just a little something for my husband.
C.O.	I see.

(sound of case being searched)

Hello, hello, hello! What's this, then? A bottle of whisky, eh?

Woman   Oh that! That's just a little something for my father-in-law.

C.O.   I see.

(sound of case being searched)

Hello, hello, hello! What's this then? A necklace, eh?

Woman   Oh that! That's just a little something for my mother.

C.O.   I see.

(sound of case being searched)

Hello, hello, hello! What's this then? A bottle of brandy, eh?

Woman   Oh that! That's just a little something for the dog . . . a Saint Bernard!

C.O.   I see. Well, Madam, I think you'd better come along with me and have a word with my superiors.

(sound of case being shut)

C.O.   This way, Madam.

(nothing happens)

Come along this way, Madam.

(still nothing happens)

Would you mind coming along with me please, Madam?

Woman   Well . . . since you ask so nicely . . .

(footsteps moving off)

Oh but what will the neighbours say? Oh dear! Listen . . . I'll do anything if you let me go!

C.O.   Anything?

Woman	Well not quite anything . . . but suppose I gave you a little something too?
C.O.	A little something?
Woman	Yes . . . a little present . . . from Italy . . . duty free!
C.O.	Madam! Are you trying to bribe me?
Woman	Oh no.
C.O.	You ought to know that the customs officers at Gitwack Airport never take bribes. No . . . you'll have to come along with me, I'm afraid.
Woman	Oh dear. But then, as we say in English, 'C'est la vie'!

(NB Either the Customs officer or the traveller can be played by a man or a woman, with very minor alterations to the script)

2 Taking a text in reported speech as their starting-point, (some examples are given below), the students can script for themselves, either orally or in writing, the conversation that took place and then act it out, possibly using a similar approach to the one described above. Although this is still a rather tightly structured exercise and the actual content of the dialogue is provided for the students, they do have a certain amount of choice in how to word this content. For example, there would be several ways of rendering into direct speech the sentence, 'The Prime Minister expressed his doubts about this.' It would be possible to say, 'I'm not so sure about that' or 'I find that rather hard to believe' or 'I'm sure you can't really mean that' or 'I have my doubts about that' etc. The teacher should make it very clear that there is no *one* correct answer, and should encourage the students to experiment with alternative ways of saying the same thing, taking care to see that the alternatives are appropriate to the situation. In the above example it would not be appropriate for the Prime Minister to say something like 'Come off it!' or 'You're joking!' even though either of these two alternatives might be perfectly appropriate in a totally different situation, say a conversation between friends. This type of exercise is

excellent practise for using the functional cue cards described later on in this chapter.

Text 1

The interviewer introduced Edward Wilson and remarked that it was always a pleasure to have the Prime Minister in the studio. The Prime Minister expressed his doubts about this and explained that not all interviews were a pleasure, nor were all interviewers as pleasant as this one. The Prime Minister invited the interviewer to put his questions. The interviewer thanked him, and began by referring to the economy. The Prime Minister interrupted with an expression of amusement and said he had thought it would be impossible to avoid that subject. However, he apologised for interrupting and asked the interviewer what his question was. Did the Prime Minister think that the cost of living would go down in the next three months, or would it continue to rise, as it was at present, steadily? The Prime Minister expressed disappointment with the question. Was the interviewer being accurate? He questioned the words 'continue to rise', and reminded the interviewer that prices and wages had now been steady for about a month. The interviewer hesitated and said he had in mind the Government's general record. This led to an angry reply by the Prime Minister that it was he who was being interviewed and not the Government.

(Templar 1976:90 & 91)

Text 2

Passenger with pole reaches breaking point

A Canadian who arrived at Heathrow with a 20-foot-long brown paper parcel over his shoulder explained that it was a fine and valuable example of delicate craftsmanship covered in carvings

– and insisted it must travel with him to Toronto in the Jumbo jet, to avoid damage.

When airline staff said the pole could not be accommodated in the passenger section, he demanded his money back and said he would travel by sea. Then he whirled round, clearing a 20-foot space and stormed out of the exit.

But as his parcel swung round it hit the door, snapped in half, and fell to the ground. After a few seconds of silent thought, he picked up the two halves and returned to the check-in desk, which allowed him to take the items on the aircraft as hand baggage.

from a popular daily newspaper

3 Half-dialogues give the student a little more leeway in that he must himself decide on one half of the conversation. Though the actual proposition is tightly controlled by what goes before and after, variety can be introduced by asking the student to be a certain sort of person, or to portray a particular attitude. Mr Bloggs, for example, could be pompous and aggressive, or oozing charm. The policeman could be grumpy and impatient, he could be very slow and painstaking and want everything repeated several times, or he could be extremely efficient and 'on the ball' and very helpful. The dialogues are intended to be used as an outline – students should be urged to enlarge upon them, and expand the written part too where they feel that this is appropriate.

Dialogue 1 Booking a room

Mr Bloggs . . . . ?

Receptionist Good evening, sir.

Mr Bloggs . . . . ?

Receptionist I'm awfully sorry, sir, I'm afraid we haven't got any single rooms left.

Mr Bloggs . . . . ?

Receptionist Yes, we've got a splendid double room. It overlooks the river.

Mr Bloggs . . . . ?

Receptionist   Yes, *all* the rooms have a bath.

Mr Bloggs . . . . ?

Receptionist   £13.50 a night, sir.

Mr Bloggs . . . . ?

Receptionist   No, I'm afraid that breakfast is extra.

Mr Bloggs . . . . ?

Receptionist   From 7.30 to 9.30. I'll ask someone to take your cases up to your room, shall I?

Mr Bloggs . . . . ?

Dialogue 2   Lost!

High Holborn Police Station

Mr Hubble   Good morning. My name is Julian Hubble.

Policeman . . . . ?

Mr Hubble   Julian Hubble.

Policeman . . . . ?

Mr Hubble   H – U – B – B – L – E

Policeman   Thank you. . . . . ?

Mr Hubble   I've lost my wallet.

Policeman   I see. . . . . ?

Mr Hubble   Just this morning.

Policeman . . . . ?

Mr Hubble   I think I must have left it on the tube.

Policeman . . . . ?

Mr Hubble   Well . . . it's quite small, and black.

Policeman . . . . ?

Mr Hubble   Leather.

Policeman . . . . ?

Mr Hubble   Yes. About £7.

Policeman . . . . ?

Mr Hubble   A few photos and some stamps.

Policeman . . . . ?

Mr Hubble   No, I'm afraid it hasn't.

Policeman . . . . ?

Mr Hubble   Oh dear, what a pity!

Policeman . . . . ?

Mr Hubble   It's 11 Marchmont Street, WC1, and the telephone
number is 3879152.

Policeman . . . . ?

Mr Hubble   I hope you do. Thank you very much. Goodbye.

3.2 Questionnaires

A questionnaire might be treated as a partially scripted dialogue
because the questioner's side of the conversation is indicated.
There are so many different types of questionnaires, forms and
surveys, however, that it is better to deal with them separately.

1   This first, very simple, questionnaire is intended to be used
during a teacher's *first* lesson with a new class of children, who
already have a basic knowledge of English. It gives the children
a chance to get to know each other quickly, and the teacher a
chance to 'size *them* up' at the same time!

Name _____

Age _____   Nationality _____

Place of birth _____   Date of birth _____

Address _____

_____

Hobbies _____

Favourite subjects at school_____

_____

Ambition in life_____

Favourite actors/actresses/singers, etc _____

_____

Favourite food _____

Things you hate _____

Happiest moment _____

Worst moment _____

Each person should be given a questionnaire. The idea is that the children should work in pairs, and then report back to the whole class on their findings (or if the class is a very large one they could report back to a group, which in turn could pass on 'potted' versions to the rest). Each member of the pair asks his partner questions and makes a note of the answers on the questionnaire itself – they do *not* fill in their own answers.

The teacher should perhaps go through a couple of the questions with the class before they divide up, to show them that the words on the questionnaire are just prompts, and are not intended as models of the actual questions that they should ask:
Name – What's your name?
Age – How old are you? ('Age?' would only be appropriate in a more formal situation, say a doctor taking down a patient's details.)
Place of birth – Where were you born? etc.
The same type of questionnaire can of course be used with adult (post-beginners) during their first session, although some of the questions will naturally be different. The teacher may wish to include questions like:
Occupation?
Reason for learning English?
Favourite reading material?
Other languages spoken? etc

Other formats can also be used:
Find out the following things about the person next to you:
His name.
Which town he comes from.
Why he decided to learn English.
What he likes doing in his spare time.

2 Students can also try out light-hearted multiple-choice questionnaires on each other. There are plenty of these to be found in magazines, which can be easily adapted, or the teacher can write his own, if he wants to focus on a particular point. Almost any tense can be pin-pointed in this way:

i   If you found a fly in your soup, *would* you . . .
a   Complain to the waiter?
b   Fish it out discreetly?
c   Walk out of the restaurant?

ii   When you last went shopping, *did* you . . .
a   Buy everything you meant to?
b   Forget at least one item?
c   Buy one or two things that you didn't really need?

iii   When you next go on holiday, *will* you . . .
a   Go somewhere you've been before?
b   Go somewhere recommended by a friend?
c   Go to Outer Mongolia?

The drawback with this type of questionnaire is that the students are presented with the entire question; they get a lot of practice in reading questions, but not in actually formulating them. If the teacher wants to practise *question* forms, he should get his students to devise their own questionnaires. As questionnaires are normally written on a specific theme the students should choose a theme and then set to work either individually or in small groups. The first time they do this some model questions, or indeed a whole questionnaire, would help them along. One suggestion would be to divide the students into groups, with each group working on a different theme. When the questionnaires are ready, each member of a group finds someone from another group to put his questions to. The groups then reform, pool their 'findings' and see if they can come up with any 'statistics' ('Only 10% of the class are smokers', 'Men seem to be more disorganised than women', 'Women buy more clothes than men each year' etc).

The sample questionnaire below is intended to reinforce the present simple tense in conjunction with adverbs of frequency and would therefore be suitable for beginners. A scoring system is also included (not to be taken too seriously!) – students may want to incorporate something of the sort when they make their own questionnaires.

How healthy are you?

1   How do you usually go to work/school?
a   By bike or on foot
b   By bus, tube, tram or train
c   By car or taxi

2   Do you play games or practise any sports?
a   Often
b   Sometimes
c   Rarely

3   Do you do exercises or go jogging?
a   Every day
b   Sometimes
c   Never

4   How many hours do you sleep every night?
a   At least seven or eight
b   Five or six
c   Four or less

5   When do you normally go to bed?
a   At 10.30 pm
b   At mid-night
c   After mid-night

6   Do you smoke?
a   Not at all
b   A little (less than 10 cigarettes a day)
c   Heavily (more than 15 cigarettes a day)

7   How much tea and coffee do you drink?
a   None at all
b   Less than five cups a day
c   At least five cups a day

8   How much alcohol do you normally drink?
a   Very little or not at all
b   A great deal
c   A moderate amount

9   Do you eat fresh fruit and salads?
a   Every day
b   Sometimes
c   Rarely

10   How often do you eat white bread, sugar, cakes, sweets and biscuits?
a   Very often
b   Occasionally
c   Very rarely

Score
Give 3 marks for every *a*, 2 marks for every *b*, and 1 mark for every *c*.
More than 25 marks: You are a health fanatic. You can expect to live until you're well over 100!

20–25 marks: You are in excellent form and able to get the most out of life.

15–20 marks: Not bad, but why don't you invest in a pair of shorts instead of buying that fruit cake!

Less than 15 marks: Oh dear!

This questionnaire is obviously aimed at adults. Suitable themes for young people and children might include 'How do you spend your weekend?', 'How brave are you?' and 'What are your plans for the future?' – (What sort of job/house/husband/family/car, etc do you intend to have?)

3   Instead of a questionnaire, the students can be given or can think up for themselves, a list of check questions to ask about a particular topic. The class is again divided into groups, each group dealing with a different aspect of the topic. 'What does the class eat for breakfast?' might be subdivided into drinks, cereals, cooked food, bread and jams, and extras. The group dealing with drinks might come up with something like:

Do you drink	orange juice? tea? coffee – black or white? If white, with hot or cold milk? With or without sugar? If with, how many? milk? hot chocolate?

Each member of the group then goes off and puts the questions to three or four people in the class (between them, the group should cover the whole class), before reporting back to his group to see if they can find any interesting trends in the information collected. Group spokesmen then relay the group 'findings' to the rest of the class so that a complete picture is built up. This exercise is a good one for practising the language of comparing:

'More people drink coffee than tea', 'The Germans have bigger breakfasts than the Spanish', 'Apricot jam is more popular than marmalade in France' and so on. Other topics which lend themselves well to this type of approach are 'Leisure Activities' (hobbies/sports/reading matter/TV programmes), 'Fears' (people/places/animals/natural phenomena) and 'Ambitions' (professional/travel/people to meet/artistic).

4 A questionnaire can be combined with a role-card which will give one of the participants extra cues, in any dialogue which involves form-filling, such as an interview for a job or opening a bank account. Students work in pairs, one has the questionnaire, the other the role-card.

A

You want a job as a waiter in this restaurant – an Italian friend, who already works here, told you that someone was leaving, so now you have come to see the manager about it. Your name is Julio García Lopez. You're 25, Spanish. You have come to London for a year to improve your English. You're studying English at a College of Further Education – 3 hours every morning, from 9–12. You need a part-time job to help pay your rent, etc.

You've just finished your degree in economics at the University of Oviedo. You haven't had a permanent job before, but you used to help your father sometimes in his little restaurant during the summer vacation.

B

You are the manager of a large London restaurant. One of the waiters has decided to leave suddenly, and you need a new one. Ask *A* questions to help you fill in the form.

Application for employment (for foreign nationals)

Name _____

Address in the U.K. _____

_____

Age _____ Nationality _____

Post applied for _____

Reason for application _____

_____

_____

_____

Educational qualifications _____

_____

_____

Record of previous employment_____

Previous relevant experience _____

_____

_____

_____

Length of intended stay in the U.K. _____

How did the applicant hear of job? _____

3.3 Cue cards

For the sake of simplicity I shall make a distinction between role-card and cue-card. A role-card tells the student who he is, something of his background, what his opinions about a given subject are, and possibly suggests a course of action that he should try and carry out. A cue-card makes more explicit reference to the actual things that person will *say*. It may give the holder 'snatches' of what he is to say, and leave him to fill it out. It may give him a choice of things to say, and leave him to choose. Or it may give him a visual or a 'functional' cue, and leave him to translate this into words. The fundamental difference between a cue-card and a script or dialogue is that a person with a cue-card has only *his* part of the conversation on that card. And this is an important difference, for he is forced to listen very carefully to what the other person says in order to be able to make an appropriate response. With a script he has no need to do this as he can see in advance what the other person is going to say.

In this section the reader will find samples of different types of cue card and these will be followed by suggestions as to how they might be used with a class.

1

A

Choose the best reply in response to B

A What do you think the weather'll be like tomorrow?

B . . . .

A I hope so.   We're going camping.

Oh I hope not.   We're going sailing.

Is it really? That's good.   We're going ski-ing.

B . . . .

A I haven't. We're going with friends.

Well there is now.

With lots of warm clothes, it's O.K.

Why don't you join us?

B . . . .

A Great!

Sure!

That's a shame!

B

Choose the best reply in response to *A*.

A . . . .

B Oh it'll probably rain again.

Well the weather forecast is good.

It could be quite nice again.

A . . . .

B Really? There wasn't much snow last weekend.

Really? Isn't it a bit cold at night this time of year?

Really? I didn't know you had a boat.

A . . . .

B I'd love to but I'm a bit busy this weekend.

I'd love to. Could Jane come along too?

Oh! That would be nice.

Often in a 'conversation' class or discussion, students who are not yet very advanced in English will stop listening to what's being said, in order to start formulating their own contributions. The above cue-cards enable students to focus on listening: they do not have to formulate what to say themselves, they only have to choose one of three possibilities. But to do this they need to catch the *key* words in what their partners says. The fact that it isn't necessary to understand every single word in order to react in the right way should be made clear to students – not just for this exercise, but as a general policy – and they should be given plenty of opportunities to practise 'gist' listening. Because of all this, the cards are probably more suitable for students whose active knowledge of English is not quite up to the level of the dialogue. They should find it both challenging and satisfying to hold a conversation which would normally be a bit beyond them. With these cue-cards, and indeed all other activities involving the use of cue-cards, it is suggested that the students work in pairs. Each member of a pair has one card, *A* or *B*, **which only he sees.** The teacher should have at least three or four different pairs of cards prepared so that the students can swap around once they have finished with one set.

2

A

(answers phone)
A Mr Appleby's surgery. Good afternoon.
B . . . .
A I'm afraid we're booked up until next month. The earliest would be February 2nd.
B . . . .
A I'm afraid that's just impossible.
B . . . .
A I'm very sorry about that, but there's really not much I can do, is there? Perhaps some aspirin would help.

B

A *(answers phone)* . . . .
B Good afternoon. I want to see the dentist.
Good afternoon. I'd like to see the dentist.
Good afternoon. I wonder if I could make an appointment?
A . . . .
B That's no good. I've got to see him now.
Can't you fit me in before then?
Couldn't you possibly squeeze me in sometime today?
A . . . .

B   Look here! This bloody toothache is killing me!
But I've got the most terrible toothache!
I know how busy Mr Appleby is, but this tooth is agony . . .
A   . . . .
B   You're joking! Listen . . . if you won't give me an appoint-
      ment, I'll come round there and just force my way into
      the surgery!
Aspirin! You obviously can't imagine how awful the pain is.
      Couldn't the dentist see me for just five minutes?
I have tried aspirin, but it didn't seem to help at all. Please
      couldn't you make an exception for me? I'd be so grateful.

Using these cue-cards, student *B* has the opportunity to choose
between any one of three different registers: he can be aggressive and rude; he can be just normally polite; or he can be super
polite and rather ingratiating. Once he has decided on the register, the student should stick to the same one throughout the
dialogue. (For clarity, the choices are given in the same order
every time.) Although student *A* has no choice in what to say,
he should be asked to vary the intonation of the words on his
card according to the type of person he is dealing with. The same
words can be said in many different ways: he should be able to
sound rude, brusque, sarcastic, sympathetic, indifferent, etc, as
appropriate. The dialogue is unfinished as it stands, and students
can be asked to work out their own ending. The ending will of
course depend very much on the sort of characters that *A* and *B*
have decided on.

3

A

You are in a post office. You have 5 letters and 7 post cards
you want to send to Italy.

1   ASK:

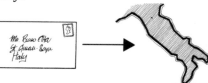

2 ASK:

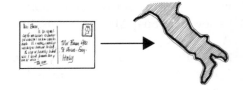

£p ?

3 ASK FOR:

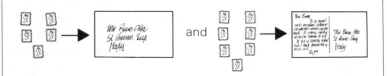

and

4 ASK:

£p ?

B

UNITED KINGDOM POSTAL RATES:

letters:	Inland	
	First class	10p
	Second class	8p
	Europe	$11\frac{1}{2}$p
postcards:	Inland	
	First class	10p
	Second class	8p
	Europe	9p

The beauty of these very simple cue-cards is that they can be used at any level, an important factor to consider for teachers, who often have little time for preparing lots of new materials. Even a class of beginners would be able to come up with:

A   How much is a letter to Italy?

B $11\frac{1}{2}$p.

A   How much is a postcard to Italy?

B   9p.

A   5 letters and 7 postcards, please. How much is that?

B   £1.20$\frac{1}{2}$.

With a more advanced class the cards might trigger off something like:

A   Can you tell me how much it would cost to send a letter to Italy?

B   All letters to Europe are $11\frac{1}{2}$p.

A   What about postcards?

B   To Europe?

A   Yes, to Italy again.

B   9p.

A   Well I'd like five $11\frac{1}{2}$p stamps and seven 9p's. What does that make?

B   That'll be £1.20$\frac{1}{2}$.

In this particular exercise, student A and student B face different problems. Although A has more to say, his questions are fixed, regardless of B's answers. B, on the other hand, can get by with saying very little, but he has to think more about his answers and work them out to fit in with A's questions. The number of situations which lend themselves well to a visual cue-card approach like this, is fairly limited. Possibilities include buying something in a shop, booking a ticket at a travel agency, making a hotel reservation and ordering a meal in a restaurant. Basically, A has a card with picture cues to prompt his questions and B has enough information to enable him to answer those questions (either on a card or on a real timetable, menu or brochure, etc).

4 *a*

A
(*B* is a stranger.)
A Get *B*'s attention. Ask him for something.
B . . . .
A Rephrase question.
B . . . .
Thank *B*.
End conversation.

B
(*A* is a stranger.)
A . . . .
B You don't understand. Ask for repetition.
A . . . .
B *You* can't help, but give *A* advice.
A . . . .
B End conversation.

b

A
(*B* is a friend.)
A Greet *B*.
B . . . .
A Invite *B* to do something.
B . . . .
A Suggest an alternative day or time.
B . . . .
A Confirm arrangement. End conversation.

B
(*A* is a friend.)
A . . . .
B Respond.
A . . . .
B Refuse. Give excuse.
A . . . .
B Accept.
A . . . .
B End conversation.

c

A
(*B* is a friend.)
A Answer the phone.

B
(*A* is a friend.)
A *(answering the phone)*

B	. . . .	B	Identify yourself.
			Greet A.
A	Respond.	A	. . . .
B	. . . .	B	Tell A about a problem
			you have.
A	Give advice.	A	. . . .
B	. . . .	B	Reject A's advice.
			Give reasons.
A	Offer alternative	A	. . . .
	advice.		
B	. . . .	B	Reject A's advice.
			Give reasons.
A	Suggest that B asks C.	A	. . . .
B	. . . .	B	Reject suggestions.
			Give reasons.
A	Add advice.	Change your mind	
		about A's first piece	
		of advice – accept it.	
B	. . . .	A	. . . .
A	End conversation.	B	Thank A. End con-
			versation.

In the above sets of cards, (based on an idea from Susan Holden) the student is given the language 'functions' he must perform – how he actually words them is up to him. His relationship with the other person is specified, as is the channel of communication (ie face to face, telephone) and he must of course take this into consideration. As the cards are written around certain functions, they could be incorporated into a lesson dealing with those particular functions. With all three sets of cards shown here, the students are required to give advice or suggest something, so it might be a good idea to practise the various exponents of these two functions (which overlap) in class beforehand:

Giving advice:
    You ought to . . .   If I were you, I'd . . .
    You should . . .   Have you tried . . .? etc
    You must . . .
Suggesting:
    Let's . . .
    We'll . . ., shall we?
Both:
    How about . . .?
    I suggest you/we . . .   Perhaps you/we might . . .
    Why don't you/we . . .   It might be a good idea to . . .
    Couldn't you/we . . .?   + straight commands.

Translated into actual speech, the dialogues might turn out in the following way:

a   A   Excuse me. Have you got a light?
     B   I'm sorry . . . what was that?
     A   Do you happen to have any matches?
     B   No, I'm sorry, I don't smoke. Perhaps that man over there
          can help you.
     A   Oh yes. Thanks anyway. Goodbye.
     B   Bye.

b   A   Hello, Sally.
     B   Oh, hi.
     A   I was wondering if you'd like to come round for dinner.
     B   I'd love to, but I'm working late tonight.
     A   Couldn't you come round when you've finished?
     B   Well I suppose I could do, really. It wouldn't be much
          before nine though.
     A   That's all right, we'll eat late. See you about nine then.
     B   O.K. See you.

c   A   Hello. Dorchester 2183.
     B   Hello Rod, this is Irene.

A   Oh hello, Irene.

B   Listen . . . I'm sorry to ring you so late, but I need some advice . . . There's this awful man and he just won't leave me alone.

A   Why don't you tell him to get lost, then?

B   Oh I can't really do that, he's rather sensitive.

A   Well can't you just pretend to be out when he calls?

B   I've tried that, but the phone goes on and on ringing. And I end up answering it.

A   Well . . . why don't you ask my sister's advice.

B   Um . . . I'd rather she didn't know about all this, actually. You see I think this guy is a friend of hers . . . makes it a bit difficult. No, on second thoughts I think I'll do what you first suggested, and just tell him to leave me alone. And if he's hurt, well, I'm afraid that's too bad.

A   Yes, that's probably the best thing. I'd tell him as soon as possible, though.

B   Oh I will, don't worry. Thanks very much. Bye.

A   Bye. See you Thursday.

Exercises involving 'functional' cues have been criticised for increasing the learning load of the students unnecessarily: they are confronted with a lot of 'metalanguage' (greet, respond, confirm, reject, etc) which they need to understand in order to do the exercise, but which isn't very useful in its own right. In practice, however, students seem to master this type of prompt with little difficulty (although it is not recommended that they be used with complete beginners). Certainly once students are working quite happily in this way, the teacher can dispense with the lengthy explanations which might otherwise be necessary to elicit specific language: the prompt is clear, and a lot of time is saved. This 'metalanguage' appears as real language in reported speech, and its meaning can be taught by using texts in reported speech. (See 'Scripted and partially-scripted dialogues'.)

4   Playing a part

At this stage we leave behind scripts and prompts, now that the student is ready to cope with situations where he is 'on his own', ie where he is not using language directed by and dependent on the teacher. This doesn't mean that students should work in a void. There are two things which can help them to achieve maximum communication. First, they need some stimulus to get them going – something concrete like a newspaper article, a photograph, or a map. They need something more than just a 'subject for discussion': 'Now today, let's talk about films' is, quite rightly, greeted with silence and blank looks. Secondly, they will communicate more freely if they have a role to hide behind. An instruction to students 'Now, I want you to work in pairs, and get angry with each other' may, if the teacher is lucky, provoke a certain amount of lukewarm and hesitant discussion. A more heated, more fluent, and more realistic interchange is likely to occur if the teacher says something like:

'You are neighbours. You left the back door open when you were hanging out the washing. Your neighbour's dog got in, devoured your Sunday joint, and was sick all over your kitchen floor.'

The suggestions which follow all involve some sort of acting a part (role-play) based on any one of a wide variety of stimuli.

What exactly is role-play? It could be defined as an individual's spontaneous behaviour reacting to others in a hypothetical situation. The essential core of the activity is understanding the situation of another person, and to do this well the 'player' needs to come to grips with the other participants' roles, not just his own. How this usually works in practice is that a player is given basic information about who he is, what he is like, and what he wants to do. He must then interact with others and relate his situation to theirs, and gain a greater understanding of the roles, the relationships, and, in our case, the language involved.

Littlewood (1975 :·202) suggests five categories of role:

1 'Inherent' roles, such as sex or age roles.
2 'Ascribed' roles, such as class or nationality.
3 'Acquired' roles, one's job, for example.
4 'Actional' roles, such as a patient, a coach traveller, or a client in a restaurant, all of which occur in the course of our active life and which are temporary.
5 'Functional' roles, such as offering help or expressing regret, which seem to coincide with Wilkins' 'categories of communicative function' (Wilkins 1976 : 41) and Halliday's 'semantic options'. (Halliday 1973 : 52)

For a learner interested in general English (as opposed to English for specific purposes), actional and functional roles will be of most use. There is a common core of actional roles which most learners must be prepared to perform creatively, such as asking for directions or buying a newspaper. But, 'performing an actional role depends on the availability of appropriate functional roles to cover each contingency, and the ability to use them adaptively in a role-making process'. (Littlewood 1975 : 204) Functional roles then, are the minimal units, the 'building blocks' of role-play, because they enter into so many different situations and because of this, a large amount of time should be devoted to their practice.

Some of the reasons for using role-play activities have already been indicated. It is time to sum them up, and add a few more.

First of all, role-play is 'learning by doing' which experiments show to be an extremely effective way of learning.

Secondly, role-play calls for a 'total response' from the player.

It asks him to communicate – to respond verbally and non-verbally – and it exploits his knowledge and experience outside the classroom, his 'common stock of knowledge'.

Thirdly, role-play can also be highly motivating. There is a game instinct involved which appeals to many people – nobody knows quite what will happen. Motivation is also increased because the students can immediately see the application of a role-play to life outside the classroom, something they cannot do with mechanical drills.

Fourthly, role-play helps provide the learner with an 'ethnography of speaking' – 'a specification of what kind of things to say in what message forms to what kinds of people in what situations'. (Hymes 1962)

Lastly, role-play can also provide the 'moment of shock' that students so often meet outside the classroom, when they find, to their dismay, that they just cannot say what they want to say. This ties in with the element of unpredictability already mentioned, which is present in a role-play activity. The students really have to listen, they cannot be sure what anyone will say, and they have to be able to think and respond quickly. They have an opportunity to cope with the 'moment of shock' inside the classroom, where the consequences may not be quite so disastrous!

There are many ways of approaching the different exercises: the language needed for the role can be practised beforehand, or the role itself can be used to pinpoint where the students' difficulties lie and what gaps need to be filled, and to indicate material to be taught in the following lessons. The class can work in groups or pairs, or as a whole, with only a few members actually taking roles, but with the role-players using ideas put forward by the rest of the class (see the restaurant role-play in the next section, page 74). In each case the material is presented and followed by suggestions as to how it might be used. These *are* only suggestions; there are many other ways of using the same material. Also, the ideas here can be applied to different materials. Teachers will doubtless want to try out other ideas if they feel them to be more suitable for their own classes.

The following sections are divided according to the different types of material that might be used to stimulate a role-play exercise in the classroom. This division is an arbitrary one, and the list is certainly not exhaustive – teachers will discover many more 'springboards' for communicative activities than the few described below.

4.1 Newspaper articles

Article 1

Family on zoo outing picked up a penguin

A mother took her daughter and friends on a day out to London Zoo last week. At the end of the day she drove them home. With four children in the back seat, all seemed remarkably quiet.

Back home in Fulwich she prepared tea in the kitchen. The children had disappeared. Tea ready, she went to find them, and eventually tried the bathroom as a last resort. There sat the children, crowded round a half-full bath. And in the bath was a penguin.

She rang the zoo, which had no knowledge of a missing penguin, and agreed to return it to the zoo. The penguin is thought to have climbed out of his reservation. It was picked up by the children and put in a duffle-bag.

from a popular daily newspaper

A nice idea for pair-work is a phone conversation with the mother ringing the zoo to explain how she comes to have the penguin and to make arrangements about taking it back.

COACH RIDE TO CHAOS

The perils of strike-bound air travel are nothing, it seems, to the hazards that can await the unwary tourist on terra firma.

For the clients of Getaway Holidays, of Rosamund Street, Kensington, a £60 round-trip coach journey to Athens last month began ominously when the bus, more than two hours late, was stopped by police in South London.

After the passengers' names had been duly noted, the coach was on its way again – push-started, of course, by the stronger holiday makers.

The German police took a dim view of speeding on the autobahn, one of the drivers fell asleep at the wheel in Yugoslavia and the coach was 36 hours late arriving in Athens. But all that was nothing compared to the journey home.

Nine hours late

Apparent over-booking led to one passenger travelling towards London in the aisle (along with all the luggage), and the coach left Athens with two drivers, but no courier, nine hours late.

By last Friday, the day on which the bus was due to reach London, the Getaway group of young British and Continental tourists and Greek travellers had reached southern Germany.

Two Germans who had booked as far as Munich dismounted on the motorway near the city. "There was some disquiet in the coach at this behaviour," said Mr Andrew Palmer, a trainee solicitor in Newcastle.

The first major breakdown occurred south of Nuremberg and a German road patrol pronounced that the bus would have to be towed to a garage. The thrifty driver, however, was able to start the engine in mid-tow whereupon smoke came through the floor into the back of the coach. It continued on its way until it was hit near Wurzburg by a car travelling in the fast lane.

"About five miles from Frankfurt, a huge cloud of smoke poured out of the engine compartment and the coach pulled into a parking place," said Mr Palmer. "The drivers poured water all over the engine and announced that the coach could not get to Calais."

Since returning to Britain by train, ferry and hitch-hiking, the coach travellers have been compensated for their additional travel expenses from Frankfurt. But some complained yesterday that from a popular daily newspaper

There are lots of ways that a teacher could use this long article.

He could get the students all working in pairs on the same thing:

For example, they might act out the conversation that took place between one of the travellers who ended up hitching home, and the man who gave him a lift as far as Ostend.

Or one of them could be the manager of Getaway Holidays, and the other the passenger who spent the return journey in the aisle. The latter has tried unsuccessfully to phone Economy Holidays and decides to go round there and complain to the manager in person. (This might be preceded by a lesson on complaints, or indeed followed up by one, if the teacher sees that his students have not got sufficient linguistic skills to handle this type of situation successfully.)

Another possibility is to have the class divided into pairs or small groups, each working on a different sequence:

1   The coach is stopped by police in South London.
2   German police stop the coach for speeding.
3   A passenger is met in Athens by a friend who has had to wait for 36 hours.
4   The drivers apologise for leaving Athens nine hours late.
5   Two Germans get out onto the motorway near Munich.
6   The coach is stopped by a German road patrol.
7   The coach is hit by a car.
8   When the final breakdown occurs, passengers are told to make their own way home.

The class then regroups, and between them they re-enact the whole story. Some chairs might be arranged to look like coach seats so that students not directly involved in the action at any given moment can act as passengers.

A written follow-up to any of these activities could be given in the form of a letter: Imagine that you are one of the Germans who booked on the coach from Athens to Munich. Write a letter of complaint to Getaway Holidays, describing the events of the journey back to Munich and the reason for leaving the bus on the motorway. Demand compensation.

NB Although most of the action takes place on foreign soil, the dialogue would almost certainly take place in English. English would be the common language for the different nation-alities involved, and it is more likely that the German police would speak English than that the British drivers would speak German. This is something that the students could consider, however. In a case where the British drivers spoke only English and the German police only German, an interpreter would be needed. The students could incorporate this into their role-play if there is a German speaker in the class. Equally, if there is a Greek speaker present, he might like to translate the drivers' apologies for the benefit of any Greek passengers who don't speak English.

When using newspaper articles, students should be given an opportunity to read the article through and clear up any points of difficulty before they embark on a role-play exercise. It is important that they are familiar with the material so that parts in role-play can be acted out spontaneously. The teacher may even want to use the article for a more intensive reading comprehen-sion exercise, either before or after the students have used it for role-play.* (Newspaper articles in general contain a lot of reported speech and are therefore very suitable for the type of exercise described on page 38.)

---

* There is another book in this series on Reading Comprehension which deals with the subject in much greater detail.

4.2 Cartoons

1

'. . . Hello . . . Hello . . . '

This cartoon (Corder 1966:56) works well if an element of mystery is introduced: cut it in half, and allow the students to see the left-hand side first. They can speculate about who the lady is phoning and why, and eventually build up their own dialogues, working in pairs. The dénouement is that much more interesting!

2

This particular Fougasse picture composition (Fleming & Fougasse 1975:10) has clear possibilities for developing the conversation between the man and the woman. Exclamations of shock and surprise, polite requests, offering to do something, can be highlighted. A rude, disdainful attitude could be contrasted with a pleasant, helpful one.

3

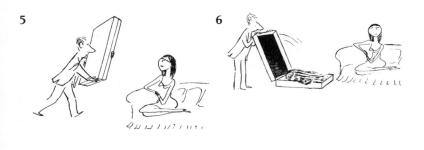

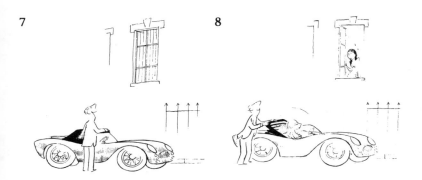

A good alternative to letting the class see the whole cartoon straight away, is to cut the sequence up and stick the individual pictures on card. Divide the class into groups of eight. Give one picture from the sequence to each member of the group. Each person must describe the picture he has and between them they must work out the story and decide on the order of the pictures. (They are not allowed to see each other's until the end, of course.) Having figured out the story, the students work in pairs and act out the dialogue:

4.3 Maps, menus and miscellaneous materials

1

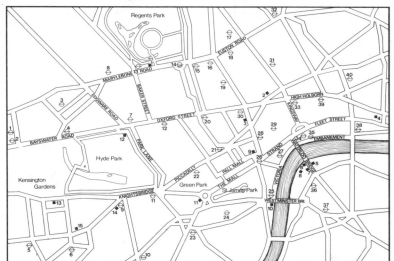

Key to Tube Stations

1. Bayswater.
2. Queensway.
3. Paddington.
4. Lancaster Gate.
5. Gloucester Road.
6. Sth Kensington.
7. Marble Arch.
8. Marylebone.
9. Knightsbridge.
10. Sloane Square.
11. Hyde Park Corner.
12. Bond Street.
13. Baker Street.
14. Regents Park.
15. Gt. Portland Street.
16. Warren Street.
17. Euston.
18. Euston Sq.
19. Goodge Street.
20. Oxford Street.
21. Piccadilly Circus.
22. Green Park.
23. Victoria.
24. St. James Park.
25. Westminster.
26. Trafalgar Square.
27. Embankment.
28. Leicester Square.
29. Covent Garden.
30. Tottenham Ct. Rd.
31. Russell Square.
32. Kings Cross.
33. Holborn.
34. Charing Cross.
35. Embankment.
36. Waterloo.
37. Lambeth North.
38. Blackfriars.
39. Chancery Lane.
40. Farringdon.

Key to Places of interest

1. Madame Tussauds.
2. British Museum.
3. Foyles.
4. St. Paul's Cathedral.
5. National Theatre.
6. Queen Elizabeth Hall.
7. Hayward Gallery.
8. Royal Festival Hall.
9. National Gallery.
10. Big Ben.
11. Buckingham Palace.
12. Speakers Corner.
13. Royal Albert Hall.
14. Harrods.
15. Victoria & Albert Museum.

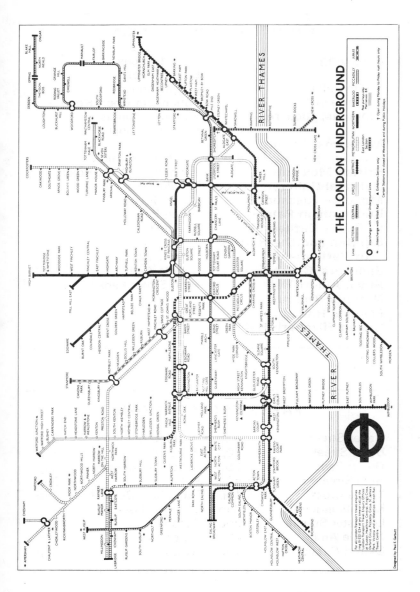

THE LONDON UNDERGROUND

Designed by Paul E Garbutt

GUIDE TO TUBE STATIONS

Shopping	Oxford Circus
	Bond Street
(Harrods)	Knightsbridge
(Foyle's)	Tottenham Court Road
Cinemas, theatres	Piccadilly Circus
	Leicester Square
Museums (Science, Natural History, V and A)	South Kensington
British Museum	Tottenham Court Road
National Gallery	Trafalgar Square
Madame Tussauds .	Baker Street
Buckingham Palace	Green Park
St Paul's Cathedral	St Paul's
Big Ben and the Houses of Parliament	Westminster
Speakers' Corner	Marble Arch
Royal Albert Hall	High Street Kensington
National Theatre **Festival Hall** **Queen Elizabeth Hall**	Waterloo

FARES FROM EUSTON

Baker Street	25p	Paddington	35p
Bond Street	20p	Piccadilly	25p
Green Park	25p	South Kensington	40p
High Street Kensington	40p	St Paul's	35p
King's Cross	15p	Tottenham Court Road	15p
Knightsbridge	35p	Charing Cross	25p
Leicester Square	20p	Victoria	35p
Marble Arch	25p	Waterloo	30p
Oxford Circus	15p	Westminster	30p

The teacher might tell the class, 'Now, just suppose you have won first prize in a competition, a weekend in London for two, staying at the Cora Hotel near Euston Station. What would you like to see most?' In order to help the class discuss, in pairs or small groups, what they would like to visit or buy in London, the teacher should give them maps with places of interest marked, and postcards (or show slides) of places to visit. He might also be usefully armed with 'Britain – Shopping in London' (available from the London Tourist Board Bookshop, see Useful Addresses), so as to be able to answer questions like 'Where can I buy a kilt?'. From this discussion a 'Guide to Tube Stations' can be drawn up – as the students offer suggestions, the teacher writes them on the board and alongside writes the nearest tube station. Each student is then given a small map of the London underground (available from London Transport, see Useful Addresses page 96) and the class practises language for buying a tube ticket and for asking and explaining how to get somewhere by tube:

'Piccadilly, please. How do I get there?'

'Take the Victoria Line to Oxford Circus and change to the Bakerloo Line', and so on.

If the teacher can manage to get hold of a large map of the London underground (also available from London Transport) so much the better, as he will be able to point out routes to the whole class and guard against the weaker students 'getting lost'!

The students then form groups of four or five. One person has a list of fares and a pile of change: he is the ticket-seller. The others take it in turns to ask for a ticket and how to get to a particular place. They give the ticket-seller a pound note, and he must give them the correct change. To add some spice to the action, the teacher occasionally slips a card to the ticket-seller: 'Give the next person the wrong change'. This means that new problems have to be coped with.

This activity serves to familiarise foreign learners with

English money and the London Underground system, and is especially useful on a short intensive course for beginners or intermediate learners who are already in Britain or who are planning to go there.

2

Dinner £4.00 incl. VAT   Saturday 28th January 7pm-10pm.

Chilled Fruit Juices
Chef's Pâté salad
Vegetable soup

Grilled Rainbow Trout Meunière
Grilled Pork Chop and Apple Sauce
Roast Duckling with Orange Sauce
Cold Meats with salad

Sauté or Creamed Potatoes
Fresh Brussels Sprouts or Buttered Fresh Carrots

Apple and Raspberry Crumble and Custard
Cream Caramel
Peach Melba
Various Dairy Ices or a selection from the Cheeseboard
   together with biscuits and celery

Wine by the glass - red, white or rosé   45p
cona coffee   30p

Last orders taken at 9.45 p.m.

Wine List

Key: Dry – D, Medium – M, Sweet – S

Bin No.		Key	Bot.	½ bot.
	WHITE BORDEAUX			
1	Blanc de Blanc	M	2.90	1.66
2	Entre deux Mers	M	2.58	1.44
	SAUTERNES & BARSAC			
3	Sauternes (Lebegue)	S	3.66	1.98
4	Barsac (Lebegue)	S	3.66	1.98
	WHITE BURGUNDY			
5	Pousse Blanche	D	3.84	----
6	Bourgogne Aligote	D	3.98	2.20
7	Chablis Première Cru Fourchaume (Domaine bottled)	D	5.66	----
	RED BORDEAUX			
8	Medoc (Lebegue)	MD	3.56	1.88
9	Château de Terrefort	MD	3.56	1.88
10	Mouton Cadet	MD	3.88	2.10
	RED BURGUNDY			
11	Beaujolais	MD	3.90	2.20
12	Mâcon	D	3.32	1.80
13	Comte de Lupe	MD	3.18	1.70
14	Paquelin Beaujolais	MD	3.42	1.84
	RHONE WINE			
15	Châteauneuf-du-Pape	MD	4.36	2.34
16	Tavel Rosé	D	3.78	----
	HOCKS AND MOSELLES			
17	Niersteiner Gutes Domthal	M	3.44	1.94
18	Liebfraumilch Hanns Christof (Dienhard)	MD	4.40	2.36
19	Liebfraumilch Blue Nun (Sichel)	M	3.90	2.12
20	Piesporter Goldtropfchen	MD	4.06	2.22
	PORTUGUESE ROSE WINES			
21	Mateus Rosé (Slightly Sparkling)	M	3.30	1.82
	YUGOSLAV WINE			
22	Lutomer Riesling	M	2.38	1.36
	SPARKLING WINES			
23	Veuve du Vernay	MD	3.46	1.92
	CHAMPAGNE			
24	Moët & Chandon	M	9.32	4.86
25	Piper Heidsieck	M	8.30	----

	CARAFE WINE	Contents		
	11° French Wine	75 cl	2.16	
	Vin Rouge, Blanc, Rosé	50 cl	1.44	
	¼ Litre Bottles – 11° French Wine	25 cl	.72	
	Vin Rouge, Vin Blanc			

This menu and wine-list have been used successfully to focus on two important language functions: ordering food and drink, and making a complaint. The situation is built up as it goes along and characters are produced as needed. The idea the first time round is to involve the whole class: to get suggestions from them, to establish any useful vocabulary and so on, before giving them the chance to go through the whole thing again in groups.

The teacher puts a table and two chairs at the front of the class and asks for two customers for the restaurant and a waiter or waitress. He gives the waiter a menu, a wine-list, and a card explaining what the various dishes are, and also telling him what dishes are not available.

Waiter's card

Chilled fruit juices
*Pâté salad
Vegetable soup

Grilled rainbow trout meunière (river fish cooked in butter)
* Grilled pork chop with apple sauce
Roast duckling with orange sauce (delicious)
Cold meats with salad

Sauté (fried), creamed (mashed, purée) potatoes
Brussels sprouts
Carrots

*Apple and raspberry crumble and custard
*Cream caramel
Peach Melba (peaches, ice-cream, and pink sauce)
Ice-cream (vanilla, chocolate, strawberry)
Cheese and biscuits (cheddar, camembert, brie)

* These things are *not* available . . . there is none left.

The action begins. The customers decide what to have, possibly ask for the wine-list, and go ahead and order. When the waiter brings the first course the teacher intervenes and says: 'Now, I want you to complain about something', and the whole class is invited to supply ideas for possible complaints:

The soup's cold.

This lettuce hasn't been washed.

The fruit juice isn't cold enough, etc.

The action then continues: the customers make a complaint and the waiter deals with it, taking suggestions from the class if necessary. Then the main course is brought. Again the teacher intervenes and asks the customers to complain, and again the rest of the class offer suggestions. Things continue in this way until some sort of resolution is reached: the customers may decide to walk out after the first course, or they may demand to speak to the manager, or see the cook, etc. In order to guard against having things just fizzle out and end rather lamely, the teacher has cards which he can slip to a student and which provide a certain unexpected element. There is a card to slip to the difficult customer when the bill arrives:

> You have no money, no cheque-book, no banker's card . . . nothing! They must've been stolen or lost on the way to the restaurant.

and one to give to someone in the class – a friend he might ring to ask for money:

> *Don't* lend this man any money – he's always wanting to borrow money from you and he never pays you back.

To make the exercise more fun various props can be used: a bottle of wine, glasses, plates, a hat for the cook, and a cloth and tray for the waiter.

After this first run-through the class discuss any problems that came up, any language difficulties (or indeed cultural problems) that they had, and the teacher may decide to work on one of those areas right away or plan to deal with it in a follow-up session. If the teacher is lucky enough to have video equipment, he can film the role-play, and then play it back to the students. This of course has a much greater impact than just remembering what the problems were. After discussion, and perhaps some further practice in difficult areas, the students move into groups to try the role-play out once again.

3

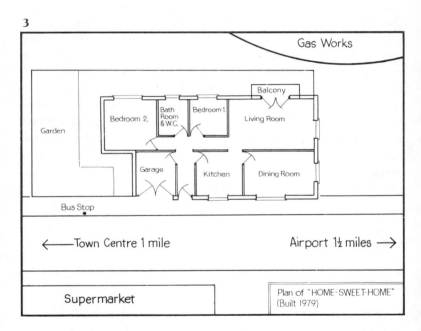

A house-plan can be used in a variety of ways. The students, as would-be house-buyers, work in groups and discuss the advantages and disadvantages of the house.

A 'jigsaw' technique (see pages 6 & 7) works very well:
Mr and Mrs Davis want to buy a house, and they each have three or four priorities, such as a large living-room, a garage, etc.

Each group of students has the plan of a different house, which they must not show to the other groups. By exchanging information about the houses orally, they work out which house would suit Mr and Mrs Davis best. (None of the houses are perfect, but one does suit them both a little better than the others.)

The last activity could lead on to a role-play where Mr and Mrs Davis talk to the estate agent about the house they've decided on.

4

National Westminster Bank Limited ♺

_____ Date

Please supply (in **Block Capitals**) the following particulars to open a | Current/Deposit/Savings/ * | account-
Loan/Personal Loan

Full names of Account (please underline surname) and/or Title of Account

Date of Birth (Care if Minor) _____

Address	Mailing Name and Address if different from address opposite
Postcode	Postcode
Residential Status	Statement Circulation
The Scheduled Territories are the United Kingdom, the Channel Islands, the Isle of Man, Gibraltar and the Republic of Ireland (Eire)	Method of despatch
Have you at any time resided in a country outside the Scheduled Territories other than for holiday or studies? **Yes/No***	Type of Cheque Book required - tick in relevant boxes Open ☐ Crossed ☐ With counterfoil ☐ Without counterfoil ☐ Standard book-25 cheques ☐ Standard book-50 cheques ☐
If **Yes** - an Exchange Control Declaration and Questionnaire must be completed	Pictorial book (25 cheques only) ☐
Description or Occupation	the book should be posted to the address/mailing address above
	held until called for
Employer's Name and Address	Reference: Name and Address and Bankers if known
I/We understand that Cheques/Credit Slips will be applied only to the account for which they have been prepared.	Special Instructions
	Reason for Opening
_____ Signatures	*Delete as applicable

This form can be used in conjunction with texts which give the participants enough information to go through the whole procedure of opening a bank account. The client is given some information, but he will have to ask a lot of questions. The bank clerk is of course given much more information – enough, we hope, to answer all the client's questions. The National Westminster brochure, from which all this information is taken, could be given to the bank clerk instead of the role-card.

Client

If you want to open an account, you go to the 'Enquiry' counter at your nearest branch and say, 'I'd like to open an account'.

The Personal Current Account isn't the only one. You can also have a Deposit Account or a Joint Account – ask the bank clerk for details.

You fill in a form, supply specimen signatures and deposit some money (£5, £50 or whatever you like). Steps are taken to find out that you are who you say you are – you must either take a letter of reference from a person who has an account with a Bank, or else give that person's name and leave the Bank to follow it up. Within a matter of days, you receive your cheque book. When you are the holder of a Current Account all kinds of services are available to you. These include a Budget Account, Travellers' Cheques and Foreign Currency, a Cashcard, and various specialist services to handle tax problems, investment and so forth. You can also apply for a Cheque Card – ask the bank clerk for more information.

Bank clerk

When someone wants to open an account, the first thing you do is to give them a form to complete. You then take steps to check that they are who they say they are. They must give you a letter of reference from a person who has an account with a Bank (any Bank will do), or else the name of that person so that the Bank can follow it up.

There are several different sorts of account:

1 *A Current Account* is a normal cheque book account.
2 *A Deposit Account* is a way of making money do some work: money in a Deposit Account earns interest.
3 *A Joint Account* is an account used by more than one person. (It can be a Current Account or a Deposit Account.) Either both parties have a cheque book to use independently or they both agree to sign each cheque.

Services available to the holder of a Current Account include the following:

1 *A Budget Account* which spreads the load of the holder's bills.
2 *Travellers' Cheques* and Foreign Currency.
3 *A Cashcard* with which the holder can draw £10 cash at any time of the day or night merely by placing the card in a machine outside the bank. These are issued free.
4 *A Cheque Card* which enables the holder to draw up to £50 at any branch of the bank (and at most branches of other banks, too). It also acts as a guarantee for cheques up to £50 made out to shops, garages, hotels, etc.

Additional information

Opening hours 9.30–3.30, Mon–Fri.

Bank Charges If customers keep their accounts more than £50 in credit, there is no charge for the bank's services.

Interest Interest is charged on a loan or overdraft.

Paying in This can be done at any branch.

Drawing out This can be done at the customer's own branch simply by presenting a cheque for the required amount, or at any other bank with a cheque card.

4.4 Role cards

The idea of having a role written on a card which only one student sees, is to ensure that he only has a part of the total information: he doesn't know what the other players will say and do, so he has to think and react quickly – any planning what to say in advance is out of the question.

Two or three students are given cards and asked to come to the front of the class to act out the situation. This can be done with the rest of the class 'in the dark', but tends to be more enjoyable if they are let into the secret: the teacher asks the card holders to go outside for a moment (with strict instructions not to show each other their cards), while he gives the others the gist of what is on the role-cards.

Role-cards may be used on their own or in conjunction with a magazine picture, text, advertisement, travel brochure, time-table, etc.

1

Husband

You've just bought a new suit. It's fantastic. The jacket fits perfectly and the trousers are beautiful. You're very proud of it. Show it to your wife.

Wife

Your husband is wearing a new suit. It's awful. The jacket's too big, the trousers are too short and the colour's horrible. Get him to take it back to the shop.

Husband's Sister

Your brother is wearing a new suit. It makes him look a bit fat, but it's a nice colour. Be kind to him, and don't let your sister-in-law be too nasty.

2

A

You've just arrived at Heathrow Airport from Amsterdam, and are waiting to go through Customs. You're smuggling diamonds in your briefcase – and the man in front of you is looking at your briefcase in a funny way!

B

You've just arrived at Heathrow Airport from Amsterdam. The man behind you has a very handsome briefcase – rather like the one you lost in Holland. Could it possibly be yours? Start by admiring the case and see if you can find a way to get a look inside – your name is on the lid of yours.

3

Mr Plant

You rang and booked a single room in this hotel two days ago. You've travelled all the way from Edinburgh to give a paper at a conference which starts early tomorrow morning. You're very tired and all you want to do is check into your room and get an early night.

Hotel receptionist

You can't find any trace of this gentleman's name. All the rooms are booked. You're going off duty in five minutes.

4

A

You are a travel agent. You think the best holiday you have to offer is the two-week package tour to Greece and the Greek Islands – it's very good value. Try and persuade this couple to go there.

> _B_
>
> You are in a travel agency with your fiancée and want
> to plan your honeymoon for next July. You really want to
> go to Spain – bullfights, flamenco, sun, wine, etc. One place
> you don't want to go is Sweden – you had a relationship
> with a Swedish lady not long ago that you'd rather forget
> about!

> _C_
>
> You are in a travel agency with your fiancé and want to
> plan your honeymoon for next July. You're dying to visit
> Sweden – you love walking, forests and lakes . . . away from
> all those people. Spain is the last place you want to go –
> too much sun, so many tourists, bullfights, etc. Besides . . .
> you had the most terrible experience the last time you were
> there!

This role-play is more realistic and more fun if the travel agent
has one or two brochures he can show the couple, giving them
information about Spain, Sweden and Greece. Whatever they
decide to do in the end, he should be able to quote them times,
dates and prices, and perhaps even make the reservations for
them.

5

> _A_
>
> You have seen this advert for a room in the paper. Ring the
> landlady to ask about it.

> _B_
>
> You are the landlady of the room advertised in the paper.
> You don't really want a foreigner in your house, but if he's
> so fond of dogs . . .

FLATS, BEDSITTERS   99

SINGLE Bedsitters for ladies only, fully equipped, fitted carpets, TV, off East St, Padmenton. – Tel 672309.

FULLY Furnished, 2-bed. Flat, suit 2 professional people, North London. – Tel 562233.

FLATS and Bed-sits in Clapham and Shoeham. – Tel 37692.

BEDSITTING-ROOM, bath-room, kitchen, suitable one person only, for care of 2 dogs, reduced rent. – Tel Man 1102.

FINCHLEY – Single furnished Flatlet. – Tel 62789.

SELF-CONTAINED furnished flat, off Chepham Road, £56.50 p.c.m. inclusive, references, garage available if required – 726894.

6

A

You are a travelling-salesman. Try to sell this . . . . . to Mrs Smith or Mrs Brown. Remember – every time you make a sale, you get commission!

B

You are Mrs Smith – a housewife. A man knocks on your door, trying to sell a . . . . . You already have one. You've begun to run your bath upstairs as you're going out in 15 minutes.

C

You are Mrs Brown – a housewife. Your old . . . . . has just gone wrong, and a man knocks on your door offering to sell you a new one.

A, the travelling-salesman, chooses one of the pictures below and tries to sell that object first to *B*, then to *C*, who are both housewives. The idea of using a picture is to give the student something concrete to focus on and make it easier for him to talk about what he is selling. Far better than a picture, of course, is

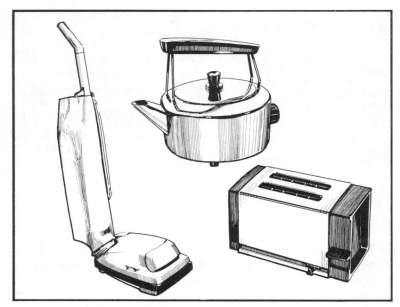

to use a real object which he can actually use to demonstrate –
a small carpet-sweeper, a toaster or a hair-dryer would all be
suitable.

If a teacher wishes to practise the language of describing and
persuading in a more controlled way beforehand, he can use
the advertisement and the suggested procedure below.

Suggested procedure:
1   Students study this advertisement in groups or pairs, and
    work out all the advantages of the car. (They should be able
    to pick out the main points without having to use the more
    difficult technical terms.)
2   They give suggestions as to how they might persuade some-
    one to buy the car if they were a car salesman.
    These language items are written on the blackboard and
    used for pair-practice.

Test drive a Ford Fiesta today

17-stage body protection process

86% all round visibility

Spacious, airy interior

Ergonomically designed rake adjustable front seats on L models upwards

Low level floor for easy loading

Advanced suspension (coil springs all round)

FIESTA S

Front air dam

Dual-line braking system (discs at front)

Widest wheel track in its class

Precise rack and pinion steering

Although few of our learners are likely to end up as travelling-salesmen, a mass of descriptive and persuasive language lurks in this situation, and can be practised in an interesting way. Having to deal with a hard-sell technique and make excuses to get away is also well worth practising.

The pictures used alongside the role-cards in the two suggestions which follow make the situation immediately obvious: they show the relationship between *A* and *B* very clearly (more clearly than words), and thus indicate which register would be appropriate. They also give the students a lot of extra information that they could bring into the dialogue.

Those observing the role-play should have an opportunity to see the picture. If the teacher has no access to an epidiascope or a photocopier, the picture should be passed around the class before the action begins.

7

A

This man's face looks familiar. You're sure you've met him somewhere before . . . Istanbul? Amsterdam? Ibiza? The Isle of Wight Pop Festival? The Munich Bierfest? . . . You must find out where it was.

B

You remember where you've seen this man before – it was at the Isle of Wight Pop Festival last year. You fell over his guitar and smashed it. You're terrified he'll remember you.

8

Wife

Your husband hasn't brought your anniversary present with him to dinner. It's obviously so special that he's hiding it somewhere . . . you're dying to see it.

> ### Husband
> You have forgotten to buy your wife an anniversary present. Pretend you're hiding it somewhere and try to change the subject. With any luck she'll forget about it and you can get her something tomorrow.

9

> ### Fiancée
> This is your dream house. It's perfect – exactly what you want. Reasonably priced too – what you've both saved should be enough for the deposit.

> ### Fiancé
> It *is* a nice house. It's a pity it's so far from your mother's as you'd really rather live somewhere near her. Don't tell your fiancée that unless you have to – give her all sorts of other reasons why the house isn't suitable.

Conclusion

By emphasising the importance of communicative teaching, I do not wish to minimise that of structural teaching: students cannot achieve communicative competence without the necessary language skills.

It is not possible to deal successfully with both the communicative and the linguistic aspect at one and the same time, but the two can be integrated by a constant change of focus: when one is brought into prominence, the other temporarily blurs into the background. With the focus on language *use*, activities such as those described on the preceding pages can be brought into play.

Many teachers realise the importance of providing for both types of practice in the classroom – I hope they will find one or two new ideas in this book to add to their teaching repertoire. Teachers who have concentrated on teaching 'structures' or 'getting through the book' and who have neglected the 'communicative' side might like to try out some of the suggestions here, (see also Practical Material, page 93) and incorporate them into their teaching programmes. They would very soon find that not only are the students getting a lot more out of their English class, but so is the teacher!

Bibliography

Abercrombie D, *Problems and Principles in Language Study,* 2nd ed, (London: Longman, 1963).

Broughton G, 'Native Speaker Insight' in English Language Teaching Journal, Vol XXXII No 4 1978.

Bruford R, *Teaching Mime,* (London: Methuen, 1958).

Campbell R and Wales R, 'The Study of Language Acquisition', in Lyons J, (Ed), *New Horizons in Linguistics,* (Harmondsworth: Penguin, 1970).

Chomsky N, *Aspects of the Theory of Syntax,* (Cambridge, Massachusetts: MIT Press, 1965).

Corder S Pit, *The Visual Element in Language Teaching,* (London: Longman, 1966).

Corder S Pit, *Introducing Applied Linguistics,* (Harmondsworth: Penguin Education, 1973).

Dickinson A et al, *All's Well that Goes On Well 2,* Teacher's Book, (Paris: Didier, 1976).

Gumperz J J, 'Sociolinguistics and Communication in Small Groups', in Pride and Holmes, (Eds), *Sociolinguistics,* (Harmondsworth: Penguin Education, 1972).

Halliday M, *Explorations in the Functions of Language,* (London: Edward Arnold, 1973).

Haycraft B, *The Teaching of Pronunciation,* (London: Longman, 1971).

Hymes D, in Gladwin and Sturtevant, (Eds), *Anthropology and Human Behaviour,* (Washington; Anthropological Society of Washington, 1962).

Hymes D, 'On Communicative Competence', in Pride and Holmes,

(Eds), *Sociolinguistics*, (Harmondsworth: Penguin Education, 1972).

La Barre I, 'The Cultural Basis of Emotions and Gestures', in Laver J and Hutcheson S, (Eds), *Communication in Face to Face Interaction*, (Harmondsworth: Penguin Education, 1972).

Littlewood W, *Role Performance and Language Teaching*, in IRAL Vol 13 No 3 1975.

Maley A and Duff A, *The Use of Dramatic Techniques in Foreign Language Learning*, in ELT Documents 77/1, (London: British Council Publication, 1977).

Rivers W, *Talking off the Tops of their Heads*, in TESOL Vol 6 No 1 1972.

Rivers W, *From Linguistic Competence to Communicative Competence*, in TESOL Vol 7 No 1 1973.

Savignon S, *Teaching for Communicative Competence*, in AVLJ Vol 10 No 3 1972.

Saussure F de, *Cours de Linguistique Générale*, (Paris: Payot, 1916).

Selinker L, *Interlanguage*, in IRAL Vol 10 No 3 1972.

Templer J C, *Interlock*, (London: Heinemann, 1976).

Ure J, *Practical Registers*, in ELT Vol 22 Nos 2, 3 1969.

Widdowson H, *Teaching Language as Communication*, (London: Oxford University Press, 1978).

Wilkins D, *Notional Syllabuses*, (London: Oxford University Press, 1976).

Practical material

Berg L, (Ed), *Folk Tales, For Reading and Telling*, (London: Piccolo-Pan, 1976). Short stories which are intended for children to *listen* to. Aimed at six to eleven year olds, the stories are ideal for the mime activity described on page 21.

Bostock P, *Dialogues and Songs*, (London: Nelson, 1974). Contains sketches which a teacher could use in the way described on pages 30 ff.

Byrne D and Wright A, *What Do You Think?*, (London: Longman, 1977). Book 1 contains drawings and Book 2 photographs grouped according to specific themes (hobbies, superstitions, disasters, etc). Both could be used to stimulate role-play exercises and both are accompanied by a Teacher's Book which gives ideas as to how the material might be exploited.

Dixey J and Rinvolucri M, *Get Up and Do It 1*, (London: Longman, 1978). Provides material to stimulate mime and fairly simple, structured role-playing activities in the classroom. The Teacher's Book gives advice on exploiting the material in the Students' Book.

English Language Teaching Documents, *Simulations, Games and Role-Play*, (London: British Council Publication, 1977). The Maley and Duff article in particular gives several ideas for games and also role-playing exercises based on mime, pictures, sounds and newspapers.

Fleming G and Fougasse, *Guided Composition for Students of English*, 2nd ed, (London: University of London Press, 1975). Some of the cartoon stories in this book lend themselves very well to simple role-play activities or short dialogues, (see page 68), particularly those on pages 16, 18 and 24.

Geddes M and Sturtridge G, *Listening Links*, (London: Heinemann, 1979). Exercises based on the idea of 'jigsaw' listening, (see pages 6 and 7), which the authors themselves have thought up and developed.

Holden S, (Ed), *Visual Aids for Classroom Interaction*, (London: Modern English Publications, 1978). Full of ideas on how to make visual aids and use them to get learners to interact with each other.

Jerrom M and Szkutnik L, *Conversation Exercises in Everyday English*, (London: Longman, 1965). Contains short substitution dialogues which are structurally based and which could be used in the intonation exercises described on pages 25 and 26.

Maley A and Duff A, *Drama Techniques in Language Learning*, (London: Cambridge University Press, 1978). Games and activities which aim to get learners using English in an interesting and communicative way.

Maley A and Duff A, *Sounds Interesting*, (London: Cambridge University Press, 1975). The different sounds on this tape give students a chance to interpret what they hear in as free and imaginative a way as possible, and to use this as a basis for further discussion or role-play activities.

Maley A and Duff A, *Sounds Intriguing,* (London: Cambridge University Press, 1979). Very much on the lines of the book mentioned above.

Ockenden M, *Situational Dialogues*, (London: Longman, 1972). Contains short dialogues which are based on situations (on a bus, in a pub) or language functions (complaining, apologising) and which also take into account appropriateness. The dialogues are very suitable for the excercises described on pages 25 and 26.

O'Neill et al., *Drama Guidelines*, (London: Heinemann, 1977). Details of activities which involve a lot of discussion in role are given, together with instructions for teachers on how to set up these situations. For every activity the age group and number of participants is specified. Although the book is aimed at native speakers of English, many of the suggestions work equally well with foreign learners.

Ramsey G, *Play Your Part,* (London: Longman, 1978). A collection of ten problems which are presented in a text. Students take on the roles of different people in the situation and try to come up with a solution. For advanced students.

Rinvolucri M, *Get Up and Do It 2*, (London: Longman, 1978). A sequel to the book by Dixey and Rinvolucri (page 93).

Scher A and Verrall C, *100+ Ideas for Drama*, (London: Heinemann, 1975). Short, simple and practical. Although written to be used with children whose first language is English, many of the ideas can successfully be used in TEFL or TESL.

Sempé, *La Grande Panique*, (Paris: Folio, 1965). Any book of cartoons in any language (the captions can always be removed!) provides interesting and humorous material on which to base role-play activities.

Taylor J and Walford R, *Simulation in the Classroom*, (Harmondsworth: Penguin, 1972). A fairly brief historical and theoretical background is followed by six simulation exercises described in detail. All these exercises are aimed at British secondary school children, but some of them, particularly 'Front Page' and 'The Conservation Game', could well be used with more advanced foreign learners. At the back of the book is a very useful directory of published simulation material, with addresses to write to.

Ready-made simulations:

Jones K, *Nine Graded Simulations*, (London: Resources Centre ILEA, 1973).

Lynch M, *It's Your Choice*, (London: Edward Arnold, 1977).

Menné J S, *Q Cards*, (London: Paul Norbury Publications, 1975).

Watcyn-Jones P, *Act English*, (Harmondsworth: Penguin, 1978).

Useful addresses

Materials such as maps, timetables, brochures, etc can often be obtained free of charge from the following organisations:

British Airways, West London Terminal, Cromwell Road, London SW7.

British Rail, Travel Centres, Enquiry Offices and 202 Marylebone Road, London NW1 6JJ.

British Tourist Authority, 64 St James Street, London SW1A 1NF.

English Tourist Board, 4 Grosvenor Gardens, London SW1W 0DU.

Greater London Citizens Advice Bureaux Service Ltd., 31 Wellington Street, London WC2.

Health Education Council, 78 New Oxford Street, London WC1A 1AH.

London Tourist Board (and bookshop), 26 Grosvenor Gardens, London SW1.

London Transport, Publicity Office, Griffith House, 280 Old Marylebone Road, London NW1.

National Travel, Victoria Coach Station, London SW1W 9TP.

National Westminster Bank, Head Office, 41 Lothbury, London EC2P 2BP.

Post Office, Trafalgar Square, 24 William IV Street, London WC2.

Index